DISCONTINUITY
OF MAN

STEPHEN HASKELL

Front Cover
Istock photo ID 938142044
Upload date March 26, 2018
Credit: Zenobillis

Paperback ISBN: 978-1-66781-638-8
eBook ISBN: 978-1-66781-639-5

Chapters

Prelude

From the ends of the earth we hear singing: "Glory to the Righteous One." But I said, "I waste away, I waste away! Woe to me! The treacherous betray! With treachery the treacherous betray!" — Isaiah 24:16 (NIV)

This is a significant passage from Isaiah. The last chapter in this book is dedicated to it. Those who will not listen will perish. We are in the end day prophecies. The sequence of events has started, and they will not be stopped. This verse in Isaiah is our final warning. Today's Christian institutional church is the Laodicean church. They have led the planet astray. Because of which we have not recognized the warning signs. Instead, these churches sing from the east to the west. The truth is not in them.

Early in 2019, *Cursed Above All Cattle* was published. It has been thoroughly rejected. A book which gave specific details on the end day prophecies was rejected. This means, people are not looking for the truth. They say they are, but they are instead looking for very refined variations of the false established narratives of the end day prophecies. To see the truth, we need to leave those violations of Daniel 8:26, 12:4 and 12:9. Entire accepted institutional church (IC) doctrines cannot be supported in scripture. Nor should the false narratives derived from the violations be believed. The IC has not accepted the truth which makes our present-day church the Laodicean church. God has told us He will spew this church out of His mouth.

As *Cursed Above All Cattle* covered the violations of Daniel, this book will expose the false Laodicean doctrines. Doctrines which are taught and believed but have no support in the truth.

CHAPTER 1:

Life Under the Premise

Today's Christian churches are teaching false doctrine on a massive scale just as Jesus told us they would. Many who attend these institutional churches (as referenced as the IC in this book) are aware that something is wrong. They see vast differences in doctrine between denominations. They see doctrines being taught differently today than in past churches. They cannot have even basic questions answered. Questions which will not be answered in church nor from any of the many online biblical commentaries for which they search for answers. They get endless amounts of hollow words and babble. Words heaped upon words with smatterings of euphemistic language about Jesus and God. Flowery speech with words with no meaning. The questions go unanswered as intended. Under the rules of tribalism, the members cannot push too far with these questions. Yes, the members of the institutional churches (IC) recognize something is very wrong, but they do not know what is wrong or to what extent they are being misled. Today's organized institutional established church has done an enormous amount of damage to God's Word.

Today's institutions are not the body of Christ nor are they the invisible church or the remnant. They are "man's" organizations. They live in man's truth. They are the ones who say, "Lord, Lord." It is through institutional church established doctrine that the leaders are leading the many astray. This established doctrine is the doctrine of the Laodicean church. Matthew 23 applies as much today if not more so then it did two thousand years ago.

Yes, some members in all Christian organizations belong to God. They are the body of Christ. Those who walk in faith are the body of Christ, not the structured organization itself.

We are in the end days. We are well into the end day prophecies. These prophecies are going unheeded because the leaders have led the entire planet astray. They have "tickled their ears" and have made God's word into myths and fables. The body of Christ needs to wake up to them. Wake up to the prophecies. Today's institutional church has become corrupted.

Jesus told us this would happen;

"Not everyone who says to me, 'Lord, Lord,' will enter the kingdom of heaven, but only the one who does the will of my Father who is in heaven. 22 Many will say to me on that day, 'Lord, Lord, did we not prophesy in your name and in your name drive out demons and, in your name perform many miracles?' 23 Then I will tell them plainly, 'I never knew you. Away from me, you evildoers!' — *Matthew 7:21 (NIV)*

"For many will come in my name, claiming, 'I am the Messiah,' and will deceive many" — *Matthew 24:5 (NIV)*

Who was Jesus speaking about? If they came in His name, they would have to be people claiming to be teaching Christianity. If not, they would not come in His name. Who are the many coming in His name? When we see who we really are and see the correct premise of why we are even here on this planet and what our rebellion of God was, it will become apparent who Jesus was speaking about.

What does claim to "be messiah" means and who claims to be messiah? Our institutional churches have led us to believe these "many" are false men teaching against the doctrine of the church. Men who teach things leading us away from salvation or leading us away from God. Who could they be?

We know about them; Jesus gave us information about them. There are "many" of them, and they "claim to be messiah." Assuming the common knowledge that few people have actually claimed to be Christ, and in those instances, they have been characterized as those on the fringe, crazy's which get no credibility and no regard from those inside the institutional church nor those outside of it. Was Jesus speaking about them? The Haley's comet prophet, Leland Jensen, made apocalyptic prophecies which never came to pass. Was that who Jesus was speaking about? Those individuals on the fringe with few followers no influence and little regard from those inside or outside of the religious community, were these the ones Jesus was referring to? Why? Men like Leland Jensen have had no influence on commonly accepted Christian doctrine. They would not seem to meet the requirement of the "many."

What does "claiming to be messiah mean? Are there many people claiming to be the Christ? Or, does that mean something else?

To fully understand this verse, we will need to make some major shifts in our way of thinking. Beliefs will need to be challenged. Things we have been taught and believed our entire lives will need to be revisited. Everything will need to be based on the scriptures.

If we go back thousands of years and look what man has done on this planet and look at what is happening today, we will see nothing has really changed. Our human nature has not changed, and the things we do have not changed. We are still living in accordance of our nature. Nothing has changed. When we understand this, we will know who Jesus was speaking about. Many will not accept the truth. Many did not accept the testimony of Jesus.

The "claiming to be Messiah" means these men are claiming to speak for God. They tell us God "whispers" in their ears, and then they spew out doctrine which is not from God but is self-serving for their own purpose, for their own business model and to maintain their own status. They may sound like they are speaking of God's glory, but they are not. They are glorifying themselves by speaking for God and making a profit from it. These are today's institutional church leaders.

". . . we do not peddle the word of God for profit. On the contrary, in Christ we speak before God with sincerity, like men sent from God." — 2 Corinthians 2:17 (NIV)

The "Many" is today's institutional church leaders. All of today's denominations are teaching "man's truth." Today's IC lives in Isaiah 29:13. Today's IC is leading the planet astray.

When Jesus spoke about the institutional church leaders in Matthew 23, He described them as "snakes and hypocrites." Nothing has changed.

Those today who are saying "Lord, Lord" have proclaimed false doctrine which cannot be supported. The established Christian doctrine of today has set up paradoxes which cannot be answered. In fact, today's leaders won't even allow questions to be asked.

We see many examples of this "claiming to be messiah" (claiming to speak for God). A short while ago, a well know man of the church, a prolific writer, came on a very well know Christian broadcast show. He claimed he had a direct communication with God. He captured what he was given in a book. He held the book up and said, "it is in here". If you buy my book, you will understand meaning of prophecies, you will hear what God has said. This man took the accepted narratives which have been around for generations, put a slightly different spin on them, twisted scripture to match what he was saying, then sold us his book. His writings and his words were just high-level general descriptions of some biblical passages. He falsely claimed the United States is mystery Babylon. If God had spoken to this man in this manner, his account of the prophecies would be drastically different from the established narratives. He would have put very specific meaning to scripture, of course he did not. The cable show could have potentially reached millions of people; he may have sold countless books. *Cursed Above All Cattle* has sold few. So, on one hand, we have a man claiming "God spoke to me" and turns around and spews out obscuration in order to sell books; on the other hand, the prophecies are spelled out in great detail but are not heard. Why? The man from the established church abides by the rules of tribalism and does not stray far from the established IC; the man with no status violated those tribalistic rules and is not heard. This man of the IC is far from alone. The "Many" stand up and say, "The Lord spoke to me," "the Lord spoke to my heart," "The spirit moved me," after which they spew out statements designed for their own glory, not Gods. Those are the ones leading the many astray. Our leaders.

Ask these men of the IC questions and listen to how they answer.

Why would God allow billions of people to come into existence, knowing ahead of time the majority of which would be destined to spend eternity in Hell? He would create many doomed to eternal condemnation in order to save a few? In man's truth, this paradox cannot be answered, indeed cannot be asked.

When this paradox is put to those who have perverted the word of God, they will say, "We don't know the mind of God," or "We cannot question the sovereignty of God." Our IC leaders will tell us of a loving God, an all knowing and just Creator, and then proclaim a doctrine which tells us the opposite. The paradox does not come from God; it comes from those "claiming to be messiah" and claiming to speak for God. Today's church has lost its way. Profoundly. We will revisit these paradoxes in the chapter where the truth about antichrist is revealed. Yes, the antichrist can now be identified. As can the question of why God has allowed the creation of all those destined for Hell.

In this country, over the past several decades, over seventy-two million unborn babies have been murdered. It's legal. Abortion is the law of the land, so no law is broken as we murder our children. This sets up more paradoxes, specifically about the age of accountability. (As well as how a "Godly nation" can commit such a vile act.)

Let's take a close look at the age of accountability paradox.

We can read what Jesus said about the "faith of a child" or when he asked the children to "come to Him," but where in anything Jesus said gives a "carveout" to children for salvation? Jesus told us, "No one goes to the Father except through Him." So, where is the carveout? Today's institutional doctrine includes the premise of this "age of accountability." It is not supported in scripture but it is taught as truth. It sets up other paradoxes. Our leaders answer this by saying they cannot imagine a loving God who would sentence a young child to an eternity in Hell, and "that's not the God I know," they say. Really? But that same loving God would create billions of people destined for eternity in Hell? God would sentence an unreconciled teenager who dies at a young age to spend eternity in Hell after being on the planet for such a whisper of time? Eternity in Hell, how is that a just punishment? All things being equal, it would not be a "just" punishment. But all things are not equal. The entire established doctrine from today's institutional church is leading the planet astray as it was prophesied to us by Jesus. They claim a "loving God," but their doctrine says otherwise. The entire premise of who we really are is not taught by the IC. My book *Cursed Above All Cattle* went into depth on this, and we will repeat some of this again in later chapters.

The "age of accountability" is a paradox in of itself. Some time ago, in a Bible study, I posed a question to the group's leader, a pastor of a small church. I asked him what happens to all those unborn babies who are legally murdered. He told me they all go to Heaven to spend eternity with God. Not only them but all the children who die before they reach the age of accountability. I asked him then why is abortion wrong. It's legal. Under this paradox, a mother who murders her unborn baby would be sentencing that child to spend eternity in Heaven. What greater love could we show than to murder that fetus. We could decide for God who goes to Heaven.

Why stop here? If we could estimate the age of accountability, we could murder our children before they reach this age. The greatest display of love we could ever show would be murdering our children. The pastor had no answer for this, but he certainly had a reaction. The same reaction we will get from all the institutional leaders when forced to support doctrines in which the Bible will not support. He didn't address the question but got angry about the question itself. He alluded that I was questioning the wisdom of God. I certainly was not; I was questioning his wisdom. This man is teaching something which is not true.

The disposition of the souls of those who die at a young age is not up to us. When knowing the truth about who we really are, we will see this to be a moot question.

Our existence started long before the foundation of the world. As *Cursed Above All Cattle* explained in detail. This verse tells us this.

"For he chose us in him before the creation of the world to be holy and blameless in his sight. In love 5 he predestined us for adoption to sonship through Jesus Christ, in accordance with his pleasure and will" — Ephesians 1:4 (NIV)

Our rebellion against God happened before the foundation of the planet. We are here because of it.

The predestination in verse 5 has little to do with us living with God in verse 4. Verse 5 tells us God had planned salvation through Christ before the foundation of the world. We rebelled before the foundation of the world; the predestination was our path to reconcile with Him. This will answer the biggest paradox of all. God did not create a planet of billions of people destined to spend eternity in Hell. We rejected Him.

This book explains the end day prophecies. They can only be seen when we see ourselves in the correct premise. If not, we will remain in darkness.

CHAPTER 2:

Dinosaurs

The American Museum of Natural History in New York City has a tyrannosaurus on exhibit. Paleontologists dug bones out of the ground and meticulously reassembled them. Each bone in its proper place. The form of this majestic beast now visible for all to see. This is a fact. It existed at some point in our past. It lived, ate, procreated and died. How old is it? When did it roam the earth?

If we stand in front of this animal with an institutional church leader and a paleontologist and ask these questions, we will get very different answers.

We need to explore this.

The paleontologist will tell us this reassembled fossil roamed the earth sixty-five million years ago. He will go into great detail about the science involved in the determination of its age. He may explain the lineage of the tyrannosaurus. He will tell us these fossils are found from the Maastrichtian age of the upper Cretaceous period to the end of the Mesozoic Era. He may mention carbon dating or radiometric dating and the science behind it. There is a great volume of science corroborating this paleontologist story.

The institutional leader will tell us a very different story. He will tell us this animal roamed the Earth within the last six-thousand years. It could not be sixty-five million years old because the Earth itself dates back only six thousand years.

In order to explore the truth about this animal, let's not enter into a futile debate over the merits of science. We know how that goes. Instead, let's look at the institutional church's history of truth.

In the not so distant past, about four-hundred years ago, the institutional church told us the Earth was flat and the center of the universe. They used verses in the book of Genesis to prove it. More accurately, they used interpretations from verses in Genesis to support this doctrine. They ignored science, dismissed it and told its members that science was wrong, evil maybe. The story was that science was "against God" and being used to deceive believers. Who in the church would oppose such doctrine after all it was a "established doctrine," which means it had to be the truth? For many generations, the church was in opposition to science on this matter. Up to the point, it could no longer be denied as to the shape of the planet and its placement in the cosmos. How is today any different? The Bible does not tell us directly the planet is six thousand years old. The verses in Genesis are interpreted to support established doctrine. While it is true the genealogy in the Old Testament puts the creation of Adam and Eve to be approximately six thousand years ago, the genealogy does not pin point the Earth's age. That is established by accepted interpretation. As the IC would not budge four hundred years ago on their false interpretation, today's IC will not budge on theirs. Indeed, if they did, it would change other established doctrine, namely the real story of creation. Today's church cannot shift to an old Earth. It would throw things off, so they will continue pushing a position which cannot be supported or will ignore the topic altogether. Something the earlier church most likely did when ships started to circumnavigate the world. None of them fell off the edge. That must have been a problem for them.

Religious man has had a very long history of being wrong. We read about it in scripture. Over and over the IC has taught doctrine which turned out to be false. From the beginning, this happened, and it has never stopped. Today is not an exception.

Let's start with Isaiah 29:13

The Lord says: "These people come near to me with their mouth and honor me with their lips, but their hearts are far from me. Their worship of me is based on merely human rules they have been taught" (NIV)

In the time of Isaiah, around 740 BC, these men did not have the truth, not God's truth. They had their own. They were practicing religion taught and based on human rules. There is no doubt these men did not believe they were teaching false things. They thought they had the truth. They may even have defended themselves by claiming to adhere to "established doctrine." After all, how could they be wrong, they were in the majority. They had to be right. Leaders of the institutional church were not teaching the truth. Their established doctrine was false but they taught it as truth.

Now let's fast forward 740 years to the gospel of Mark.

Then he said to them, "The Sabbath was made for man, not man for the Sabbath." — Mark 2:27 (NIV)

Think carefully about this statement Jesus made to the leadership. Thirteen-hundred years before Christ made this statement, Moses walked down from the mountain with the Ten Commandments. How could these leaders be teaching a basic commandment wrong? For how many generations were they teaching this wrong? This is not the only commandment Jesus corrected them on; they were also teaching "honor thy mother and father" incorrectly as well. Their established doctrine was false but they taught it as truth.

Four hundred years ago, the largest Christian church on the planet taught a false doctrine. Much like the leader standing in front of our tyrannosaurus, the IC leaders would speak with confidence in their belief as to the shape of the Earth and the placement in the cosmos. They would dismiss science as much as today's institutional leaders do. They were wrong then; they are wrong now. The established doctrine was false but was taught as truth. Today's leaders will use guilt and shame if a parishioner questions their interpretation of the seven-day creation. After all, it is a staple of today's doctrine, so it has to be right. It's a wrong interpretation. Man is always wrong.

Throughout the Bible, man has rejected God. Man has taught man's truth as God's truth. Why is today any different? When did it change? I put this question to an institutional leader some years ago. His answer was, "Christ changed all that." I asked him when? Did it change after they killed Him? After they tortured, imprisoned and killed the disciples and apostles? After the Catholic Church convicted men of heresy for not believing a false doctrine? Christ did not "change all this" and man is still doing what man has done from the beginning.

Christ did not change man's nature. It has not changed. Today, we have church leaders running multimillion-dollar operations. They lead mega churches. They make millions selling books. They have status and many follow them. How could they be wrong? After all, they follow established doctrine.

Who are these men and what has the Bible told us about them? As it turns out, the scriptures tell us a great deal about today's institutional church leaders.

"For the time will come when people will not put up with sound doctrine. Instead, to suit their own desires, they will gather around them a great number of teachers to say what their itching ears want to hear. 4 They will turn their ears away from the truth and turn aside to myths." — 2 Timothy 4:3 (NIV)

The institutional church leader standing in front of the tyrannosaurs fulfills this prophecy. In order to satisfy the "established doctrine" of the age of the Earth which has been falsely taught for many generations, he tickles their ears and turns to myths and fables. This man will ignore science as much as the leaders did four hundred years ago and teach myths. Many of these leaders do not believe in the young Earth but they will not stand up to the established doctrine for fear of losing their people or their status. I suspect there was a time when the Catholic leaders did the same. Tow the party line even know they didn't believe it themselves.

Let's continue and hear what Jesus told us about todays' IC leaders:

"For many will come in my name, claiming, 'I am the Messiah,' and will deceive many" — Matthew 24:5 (NIV)

Jesus told us of todays' leaders. These men coming in His name are members of Christian churches. They have to be or else they would not come in His name. They will claim to be messiah, which means they will speak for God. How many of these men tell us Jesus whispers in their ears or otherwise tell us they are getting direct communication with God? They will say things like "the lord spoke to my heart" with great emphasis, and they will sound sincere, but their words don't glorify God; their words glorify themselves or the false doctrine they spew out. Even saying such a statement glorifies themselves. They are speaking for the messiah. They are leading many astray. These are our leaders.

Jesus told us more about them in the gospel of Matthew;

"You snakes! You brood of vipers! How will you escape being condemned to hell? Therefore, I am sending you prophets and sages and teachers. Some of them you will kill and crucify; others you will flog in your synagogues and pursue from town to town." – Matthew 23:33–34 (NIV)

This applies today to our leaders as much as it did two thousand years ago to those leaders. Nothing has changed. Man has not changed. Our nature has not changed. These men put themselves above others. They will not answer questions. They will not defend their doctrine. In their commentaries, they go on and on and say nothing. They evade even basic questions and speak in fluff and euphemisms. They are the ones who say "Lord, Lord."

"Not everyone who says to me, 'Lord, Lord,' will enter the kingdom of heaven, but only the one who does the will of my Father who is in heaven. Many will say to me on that day, 'Lord, Lord, did we not prophesy in your name and in your name drive out demons and in your name perform many miracles?' Then I will tell them plainly, 'I never knew you. Away from me, you evildoers!'" – Matthew 7:21–23 (NIV)

These are our leaders. They tout established doctrine and lead the many astray.

There is a great danger happening today. This man standing in front of the tyrannosaurus who is telling us it is six thousand years old is also telling us other things which are not true. He is telling us the mark of the beast is a litmus test for believers in the end days. He is telling us about a man, this antichrist, will come along in the end days and try to rule the world. He tells you the enmity in the book of Genesis is between Christ and Satan. He is wrong. The doctrine is false. This book, as did *Cursed Above All Cattle*, deciphers the prophecies. Who will listen?

". . . blessed are those who hear it and take to heart what is written in it, because the time is near." — Revelation 1:3 (NIV)

CHAPTER 3

Why Are We Here?

My father died recently at the age of eighty-one. I was with him when he died. Before he died, he said something which struck me. He said, "It's gone by so fast." An eighty-one-year-old man said it's gone by so fast. If an eighty-one-year-old would make such a statement, what about a young man dying in battle or a teenager dying of a disease or in a car accident. If eighty-one years goes by fast, what about fifty or twenty, or seventeen?

Our days may come to seventy years, or eighty, if our strength endures; yet the best of them are but trouble and sorrow, for they quickly pass, and we fly away." — Psalm 90:10 (NIV)

It leads to what seems to be a very basic question of our existence. Why are we here? Why did God put us here on this planet for such a brief period of time?

If we look at how the institutional church answers this question, we will see a remarkable truth about our IC. The entire institution is teaching something dramatically false. Man has indeed fallen short. While living in the current church doctrine, being part of it, it may be difficult to see where it falls short. As it was for the church members believing the earth was flat and the center of the universe. If we remove ourselves from the current church tribalism, we will get a much clearer picture of who we are and why we are here. In fact, we will see a great many things more clearly including the prophecies. Being on the outside, looking in, we will see the remarkable hypocrisy our church leaders live in. They exert a tremendous amount of control over their sheep. Members of our organizations are living in blindness. Many of these members realize something is wrong. They may not be able to pin point it or define it exactly, but they sense something is wrong. Not until a church member leaves the Laodicean doctrine will they come out of the blindness. While in it, they cannot question the doctrine, the beliefs or the theology of that IC. It's the control of these leaders which prevents the members of the remnant from seeing them for what they are. They are the ones leading even the elect astray. In Matthew 24:24, Jesus told us they would deceive even the elect if that were possible. Today's institutional Christian church is the church of Laodicea. It has greatly damaged the remnant. They are killing the truth as did the IC two thousand years ago. Until the remnant understands the damage being done by our church leaders, the death to truth will continue.

But if your eyes are unhealthy, your whole body will be full of darkness. If then the light within you is darkness, how great is that darkness!" 24 "No one can serve two masters. Either you will hate the one and love the other, or you will be devoted to the one and despise the other. You cannot serve both God and money. — Mathew 6:23 (NIV)

This verse in Mathew eviscerates today's Christian organizational Laodicean church. All denominations. The light in the body are the leaders teaching things which are not true.

Why are we here on this planet? If we ask today's Laodicean church, their doctrine will set up an endless number of paradoxes. The IC does have an answer from established doctrine. It will not hold up to the truth because it does not take into consideration of when our rebellion against God really started. If we cover verse by verse, the churches rational as to why we are here, we can see the paradoxes as well as its false doctrine.

Their narrative, which is false, basically tells us that Adam and Eve were put on this planet to worship God and to follow Him. To be perfect and live in harmony. They and their descendants would live in this perfect world without sin. We would all worship God and be a pleasure to Him. But something bad happened, they surprised God and fell when they disobeyed Him severing the spiritual connection with Him. The sin of Adam and Eve essentially changed the trajectory this planet was on. It threw God's plan off because of their disobedience. Adam and Eve would be cursed as well as all the following generations. Because of this sin, they and all the generations that followed would need to reconcile to God because of Adam and Eve's disobedience. This is the general doctrine on this. It is false doctrine and will set up these paradoxes.

In chapter five, we will identify the antichrist. In order for us to understand who the antichrist is, we will need to understand some of the paradoxes the institutional church has given us.

If Adam and Eve were without sin, why would God tell them not to eat of the tree of knowledge but then put it within their reach? Why would He have allowed the serpent to tempt Eve? Why would God not have stopped Eve from eating from the tree?

The IC has no answer for this, no real one. Apparently, it is a test that God gave them, one in which they failed. Now they and all their descendants will pay for this. Does this really make sense?

Why would God punish us for their sin and condemn billions of people to spend eternity in Hell? It's a paradox. That is not what happened. Our rebellion against God started before the foundation of the planet. True Adam and Eve set things in motion when they disobeyed God but that was a foregone conclusion. Adam and Eve did not surprise God. Us being here in our sin was the plan from the beginning. It started long before God made the planet. It's why He made the planet.

There should be no doubt that the plan for salvation was made for us before the foundation of the Earth. Why? God would have had to know ahead of time what would happen. But He did it anyway? Why would God subject this planet to immense pain and suffering for thousands of years and condemn billion of souls to eternity in Hell? I asked this question in the last chapter. Why would a loving God do such a thing?

In *Cursed Above All Cattle* as well as the previous chapter, a mention was made to our existence before the foundation of the planet. It is scriptural. Ephesians 1:4 tells us that we lived with God before the foundation of the world. The premise itself does not conflict with the Bible or with God. If you believe that we did exist prior to this Earth, and if you believe that we did rebel against God prior to the foundation of the world and further believe that we are here because of that rebellion, then the entire Bible now makes sense with no paradoxes. God's loving nature makes sense and would not conflict with the questions which cannot be asked. The paradoxes. It also blows wide open the prophecies which have been hidden from us until now. If you believe this and understand it, you will understand why God built this planet and put us on it. We rebelled against God; it is us who wanted to live outside of the embodiment of God. God gave us our wish. Here we are. In the understanding of this all the questions which are not allowed to be asked are now answered. No paradoxes.

If you do not believe this, then God cannot be the loving God which is preached by the IC. In this narrative of the IC, our Creator would have to be either incompetent or heartless or cruel.

I have supported my narrative by using scriptures. The entire book *Cursed Above All Cattle* supports the premise of our pre-existence.

In the rest of this chapter, let's see how the IC supports its narrative. The question was asked, "Why did God create us?" We know what the IC narrative is and now let's go through and see how they support it.

"Everyone who is called by my name, whom I created for my glory, whom I formed and made." — Isaiah 43:7 (ESV)

The question is, "Why did God create man?" The above verse is the institutional churches primary reference to answer this question. It's an absolutely remarkable response. In order not to seem biased, I will add a few of the other favorite verses the IC uses to answer this question. In order of popularity. None will answer the question. None will support their narrative. All set up the paradox.

This verse from Isaiah, how does it address the question, "Why are we here?" Think about this verse, what does it really tell us about our creation? It tells us God created us, but we already know that. By answering the question in this manner, it tells us a lot about our institutional church. It does not really answer the question. It deflects the question. It answers a question not asked. Why? Why would the IC be evasive on such a basic question? We will find out in chapter 5 when the antichrist is revealed.

Why have we always assumed our soul (or spirit) or that part of us not restricted to the physical was created in uterus, during our physical birth? We acknowledge our spiritual essence will continue after our physical death but never speak about that spiritual existence Ephesians 1:4 tells us of. The Bible does not tell us our spiritual existence came into being during physical birth. It is established doctrine. As was the flat Earth. It is equally false.

It seems like heresy too many to even broach the concept that we existed before the foundation of the planet. The concept itself is supported greatly in scripture, and it certainly does not conflict with it. Not one verse in the entire Bible states we came into being at birth. It is an assumption. A false one. If it is something you believe, then you will never be able to answer the paradoxes.

When the IC uses the above verse to answer the question as to why God created us, they display their very weak and unsupported premise. The IC today, as in the past, is doing a great deal of damage to the truth.

Then God said, "Let us make man in our image, after our likeness. And let them have dominion over the fish of the sea and over the birds of the heavens and over the livestock and over all the earth and over every creeping thing that creeps on the earth." — Genesis 1:26 (EVS)

If Isaiah 43:7 is the primary verse to support the answer to the very basic question as to why God created us, this is a close second. Again, how is it that this verse answers the questions to why we were created? We will see a common trend; they have no answer. Our IC today is the Laodicea church. Today's established doctrine has lulled the believers to sleep. The sermons and church dogma are designed along business models, and they spew out euphemisms about Jesus and God. The sermons are superficial and shallow.

Little truth is being taught. We ask the IC why God created us, and they spit out this verse and tell us to move on. They tell us to ask no further questions about this or we will be challenging the sovereignty of God. Thus, such a basic question will go unanswered and truth dies a bit. The lukewarm church goes on its way. The truth is concealed, the prophecies remain hidden and the parishioners are held in line by the rules of tribalism. At the end of this chapter, we will revisit this verse and answer the question correctly.

"And to bring to light for everyone what is the plan of the mystery hidden for ages in God who created all things, so that through the church the manifold wisdom of God might now be made known to the rulers and authorities in the heavenly places." — Ephesians 3:9-10 (ESV)

This is an interesting response to the question. How does this come close to answering why God put us on the planet? It sounds like the response is "so we can receive salvation." So, God would make the human race in order to save a small number of them and condemn the rest to an eternity in Hell? Now we are back to the cruel God. The one the IC describes to us, while they tell us the opposite.

The IC today is leading many astray. Their answer to this question is a good example of something. A church member may have a question and seek out a church leader for an answer. Like "why are we here?" which seems to be a legitimate question. This question, as of many, will get a certain response. In the previous book, we spoke of this. I called it the "response technique." This is how it works; a question will get asked, and the IC leader will spew out what appears to be an unrelated response. The member may re-ask the question, and the leader will imply the question has been answered and further imply it's the members fault for their inability to understand the answer. Under the rules of tribalism, the member may acknowledge the answer by saying something to the effect of "Ahh, now I see." Of course, they don't see because the question was not answered. If that member persists with asking questions, they will be discouraged from doing so by church leadership. The question has gone unanswered. The paradox has gone unsolved because we existed with God before the foundation of the planet. The IC is misleading the many.

"The people whom I formed for myself that they might declare my praise." — Isaiah 43:21 (EVS)

Some believers point to this verse, but if it's their answer, it will still not address the paradox. If an institutional church leader uses this verse to answer such a basic question, they will still need to address the paradox of why God would create us knowing beforehand the majority would not be saved. Was He really willing to condemn the majority to Hell in order for a few to praise Him?

This is a remarkable response to the question, not so much because of the deceit, but because it is taken out of context with the surrounding passage.

These above passages are the most popular by the IC to answer the basic question. There are more but become less and less relevant as we go down the list. It is a waste of time hunting down this answer from the IC. You will not get one. Man's church is not teaching us the truth about who we really are.

In an effort to address this paradox, some will mention free will. Something not directly addressed in the Bible. It is an interesting response. Some people who call themselves believers will very condescendingly throw out the topic of free will. They will impugn non-believers by saying they have the free will to choose not to reconcile with God. Did God not know He created us with free will?

After which He would then not directly intervene with us on the planet, allow us the choice and then condemn the majority to Hell? Why would God allow this? Does this sound like something a loving God would do?

Jesus said,

"Enter through the narrow gate. For wide is the gate and broad is the road that leads to destruction, and many enter through it. But small is the gate and narrow the road that leads to life, and only a few find it." — Matthew 7:13-14 (NIV)

Ephesians 1:5 mentions the predestination of Christ. Revelation 13:8 and 17:8 mentions those that did not have their names written in the book of life before the foundation of the planet. God knew the vast majority of people on this planet would not reconcile with Him. He knew this before the foundation of the planet. So, the question they will not answer and the question you are not allowed to ask is, why did God create us in the first place? Why did He allow us to come into existence knowing full well the majority would spend eternity in Hell? It's a man-made paradox.

So, why are we really here? Why did God put us on this planet? Why do we need salvation? Why has God left us alone? Why is there so much pain on the planet? Why does God not intervene and stop the pain and suffering? All these questions can be answered from scripture. They will not be understood from those living in Laodicean. They will not be seen to those living in the man's truth of established doctrine.

For he chose us in him before the creation of the world to be holy and blameless in his sight. In love — Ephesians 1:4

Then God said, "Let us make mankind in our image, in our likeness, so that they may rule over the fish in the sea and the birds in the sky, over the livestock and all the wild animals, and over all the creatures that move along the ground." — Genesis 1:26

"For God knows that when you eat from it your eyes will be opened, and you will be like God, knowing good and evil." — Genesis 3:5

And the LORD God said, "The man has now become like one of us, knowing good and evil. He must not be allowed to reach out his hand and take also from the tree of life and eat, and live forever." — Genesis 3: 22

This collection of passages answers the question of why we are here. We will go through each of these and explain something which is not accepted by "established doctrine."

The verse in Ephesian's tells us we lived with God before the foundation of the planet, which we did. Something happened. We rebelled against God. We wanted to live as our own gods, independent of our Creator. The Archaios serpent, the entity of Satan, was the leader of our rebellion. And here is the secret. This entity, Satan, will not be on the planet until the end. Revelation 12 tells us this. More on this in a minute.

We need to take a very close look at Genesis 1:26, "Let us make man in our image." This is extraordinary important. It is before Adam and Eve disobeyed God. What God is telling us is that He gave us our wish, to live unrestricted from Him. We needed to sever our spiritual connection with God in order to do this. We wanted to live as our own gods, so God let us. It is why we are here. It is why God made this planet. There was a restriction, many actually. Verse 3:22 alludes to one. Our human lives have a limited amount of time. The entire process was for us to live without God, unbiased from the time before.

This unbiased life, the knowledge of it, will answer another paradox. Why does not God make a direct connection with us? Make himself known? We will speak to this later in this book. There is rational for it. Why does God not stop the pain and suffering on this planet? That was addressed in *Cursed Above all Cattle* and will again be spoken of in this book. We have been given what we had asked for. Life as our own god.

Here is the secret. The entity of Satan, the Archaios serpent, the leader of the rebellion, has been on the sideline as well. He has had very little interaction with us as God has had very little interaction with us. Again, this will be explained in this book. Satan will not get thrown out of Heaven until after the apostate. We are there.

CHAPTER 4:

The Nature of Satan

Lucifer, the dragon, the devil, Satan and the serpent. Just who is Satan?

The better question might be, what is Satan? The teaching on Satan has changed drastically over the generations. It has evolved, morphed even. The way Satan is taught today, even in Christianity, is much different than it was taught generations ago. Today, Satan is taught and understood as a singular entity. The fallen angel, the red man with a pitch fork. He hides behind every tree; he is everywhere, waiting to tempt us and make us fall. To destroy us. Is this really who Satan is, what Satan is?

In today's institutional church, Satan has to be taught this way, as the singular entity trying to ensnare us at every turn. It is of course a myth like most of today's IC doctrine.

Today's doctrine fulfills prophecy:

"They will turn their ears away from the truth and turn aside to myths." — 2nd Timothy 4:4 (NIV)

In today's established doctrine, the devil, the singular entity, Satan, is taught as a mythical fallen angel of God. Not much mention of the fact from the IC that Revelation 12 tells us the ancient serpent does not get kicked out of Heaven until the end days. This fact places a very large hole in their doctrine. It fulfills this prophecy in the book of Timothy. We'll get to Revelation 12 in chapter 9.

According to this established doctrine, there are essentially three forces in play on this planet. The good, which is God, Jesus and the Holy Spirit. The bad, which is Satan and the fallen angels; and the innocent, the humans born in the middle of this spiritual war. The humans will have to pick a side in this battle. We will reconcile with God or spend eternity in Hell. But this sets up a paradox. Actually, it sets up many paradoxes as the prelude to this book alluded to. In this scenario, why would God not be better at explaining things to us? Why would we have to search for Him? You would think a loving God, the Creator of the universe would be a little better in proving to us His existence. After all, our eternal life is at stake. Would God leave that up to chance?

By understanding who we are and why we are here, we will understand why God does not send angels down in our sight. We will understand why He does not show Himself to us or directly prove His existence. We are here to live in our separation from Him; that was our choice not God's. If God were to directly prove His existence to us, it would undermine the entire purpose for us being here. Another paradox. Why does God not directly prove His existence? The IC will not answer this, certainly not in a way that holds truth. They can't because of the false doctrine that our existence on this planet was involuntary. It was not.

The established church doctrine of Satan is completely incorrect and cannot be supported in scripture.

Today's Christian doctrine has Satan wrong, our origin wrong, the serpent in the book of Genesis wrong. What else do they have wrong?

From the previous book, *Cursed Above All Cattle*, we looked at who King Tyrus was in Ezekiel 28. The King of Tyre was called a mortal man three times by God, three times! The IC still twisted it into Tyrus was Satan. They had to support a false narrative of Tyre to support the false narrative of Satan as well as a false narrative of who we are. The false narrative removes our guilt and puts it on Adam and Eve. The false doctrine hides who we really are. There is no evidence at all in scripture that the King of Tyre was Satan or possessed by Satan. This false doctrine was derived by a complete lack of understanding of what Satan is.

The Bible makes many references to Lucifer, the dragon, the devil, the serpent and Satan. In order for us to understand the end day prophecies, we will need a much better understanding of who "The spirit of Satan" is and who we really are. Satan is not the red man with the pitch fork standing behind every tree waiting to tempt us and lead us away from God. In fact, Satan will not be kicked out of Heaven until Revelation chapter 12 and after the woman flees to the wilderness. That will be explained later in the book. No matter how you look at Revelation chapter 12, Satan could not have been thrown down in the book of Genesis. Even if you believe the false doctrine that the woman in Revelation 12 is Israel, Satan would not have been thrown down for four thousand years after Adam and Eve were evicted from the Garden of Eden. The woman is not Israel, and "The Satan," the Archaios serpent," will not be thrown down until the end days, six thousand years after the eviction. They can't support their doctrine without twisting scripture. This paradox of King Tyrus and when the devil get thrown out of Heaven is set up by false established doctrine.

When the scripture references Lucifer, the dragon, the devil, Satan or the serpent, it is not a reference to a singular entity, not always at least. There are instances in which it was. In Job, Satan spoke with God, but Satan was not in the flesh; remember, he came with God's angels. He could not have been in the flesh. Contrary to established doctrine, Satan had not been cast out of Heaven yet. We see Satan again in the gospel when he tempted Jesus. Again, he was not in the flesh. We see Satan, the singular entity, again in Revelation 12. Most of the references to Satan, the serpent or the dragon, are actually a reference to something else. The reference is to us, our nature or the nature of the rebellion. Our rebellion and not Adam and Eve's. When Jesus said to the Jewish leader in John 8:44, "you belong to your father Satan," it was a reference that the man was still living in the embodiment of the rebellion. He had not reconciled with God. Certainly, Satan was not that man's biological father. We will look at other references which are about us. The references to the dragon are a reference to the collection of the fallen natures.

To understand how this Satan has been taught, we will look at how the Jews looked at this Satan. In a Jewish online publication, My Jewish learning by MJL and MJL Admin, it states:

Satan appears in the Bible, was discussed by the rabbis of the Talmud and is explored in detail in Jewish mysticism, or Kabbalah. In Hebrew, the term Satan is usually translated as "opponent" or "adversary," and he is often understood to represent the sinful impulse (in Hebrew, yetzer hara) or, more generally, the forces that prevent human beings from submitting to divine will.

This is the correct understanding of Satan, the serpent and the dragon. These are references to our rebellious natures against God. The spirit of what opposes God and not just always that singular entity. This "spirit" is our nature, our fallen and rebellious nature against God. It's us. Essentially, we are Satan.

In *Cursed Above All Cattle*, we went into great detail to explain who the serpent in Genesis 3 was. It was us. God was speaking to us in Genesis 3. The enmity is between male and female. It was put there by God as a protection. An understanding of this puts a major crack in the false teaching from the church as Satan being strictly a singular entity. We are not innocent.

Let's go into scripture and unravel this Satan. Starting in Genesis 3. God spoke to the serpent:

"And I will put enmity between you and the woman, and between your offspring and hers; he will crush your head, and you will strike his heel." (NIV)

In our first unraveling of the serpent, we need to understand salvation through Christ was predetermined before the foundation of the Earth. We know this because God told us. The spirit of God and the spirit of Satan are and have been in opposition since before the foundation of the planet. So why would God "put enmity" between two opposing spiritual forces? The IC teaches this enmity is between Christ and Satan. How could this be? It's a future statement, "will put." Why would God put enmity between two opposing spirits in the future? It's a paradox, and it's false. Enmity already existed between the opposing forces long before the planet was formed and long before this enmity was put between men and women.

Who is the serpent's offspring? Is the serpent the serpent's offspring? When this paradox is put to the IC, they will refer to John 8:44, "your father the devil." This is completely taken out of context. We've already seen what that reference was. If the enmity was between Christ and Satan, there would be a conflict in this verse;

in one case, the serpent's offspring would correlate with a spiritual affiliation to Satan, and in the other "offspring" in the same verse, it would mean a physical offspring, Christ. Current doctrine tells us the woman is Israel, and the offspring is Christ. This is not supported by scripture. It's a paradox. It's also false. The enmity is between male and female. Yes, the "he" in this verse is a reference to Jesus. This is validated in another scripture. The woman is not Israel, and the offspring are not Christ and Satan. Many biblical translations use the word seed instead of offspring.

The enmity in this verse is strictly between male in female. Specifically, between unlike natures. Again, God put that in as a protection. Many older married men or those who have counseled couples most likely have a great deal of understanding of the enmity. It's that thing we do not speak about. Anything which speaks to a negative component of the female nature is off limits for conversation. Cultural conformity will not allow us to acknowledge the enmity. In doing so, large amounts of scriptural references to the female's nature is as well out of bounds.

The serpent in Genesis was us. God was speaking to us. The paradox dies and so should our false perception of Satan. We are the ones who rebelled against God. It's why we are here, and it's why we are not innocent victims. The Jewish concept of Satan was taught correctly.

This is just the very beginning to unraveling the "dragon."

Let's move to the book of Corinthians:

"Do not deprive each other except perhaps by mutual consent and for a time, so that you may devote yourselves to prayer. Then come together again so that Satan will not tempt you because of your lack of self-control." —1 Corinthians 7:5 (NIV)

This is a fascinating passage. Let's examine it closely to put meaning to it. Specifically look at this; "So that Satan will not tempt you." The implication is that if a female turns down her husband for sex, he will look elsewhere, therefore, tempting the man into an adulterous relationship. Satan will do this? So, who is Satan? Let's do the math on it. Today, there are over seven billion people on this planet; at the time Paul wrote Corinthians, there were about 300 million people on the planet (the number is not all that important). With billions of couples in relationships today, and if this verse still applies, will Satan will be monitoring all our relationships? So how big is the red man with the pitchfork? Would he be so strong and omnipresent as to interfere with billions of couples simultaneously? How would Satan be able to monitor the sexual activity of all these couples? Knowing a husband is not having relations with his wife and then tempt him to have an affair with the girl at the coffee shop? How would Satan be able to communicate with that girl at the coffee shop and put it in her mind to tempt that married man, causing him to fall? Wow, Satan would have to be awfully powerful. In between causing hate, mayhem, murder and general chaos on the planet, he has time to dive into our personal intimate lives? Who is this Satan, and what are his limitations?

In our traditional view from the established doctrine of Satan, how would he be able to exert this type of influence and have this amount of secret information? If not, what else could this verse mean? Who or what else could this Satan be?

The answer comes from the Jewish doctrine of Satan. The "Satan spirit" which opposes God, an adversarial spirit against God, that thing which separates us from God. It's that spirit within us and not an external singular entity. This spirit is our fallen nature and that which opposes God. The Jews have this correct and the established Christian doctrine does not. If we look at it the way the Jews teach

35

Satan, everything will fall into place and many more scriptures will start to take on meaning like what Jesus said to Peter. We'll get to that.

Understanding what this Satan "spirit" is will allow us to understand that God was speaking to us in Genesis 3, and we are that serpent. This verse in Corinthians should now be clear. What tempts this man is not Satan the singular entity or the red man with the pitch fork but the man's nature itself. That nature, the fallen rebellious nature, which opposes God is what will tempt this man. That Satan is a reference to our own nature. It's a reference to us.

The institutional church is teaching many false doctrines as Jesus told us it would. The rational to explain this about Satan is very important. If we understand that references to the dragon, Satan, the serpent or other references to Satan are often referencing to our nature, then we will be able to unlock the end day prophecies. Otherwise, we will be blind to them.

I will never deny the existence of Satan as that singular entity; he apparently does exist as the Archaios serpent. Revelation chapter 12 tells us about this entity. The Archaios as interpreted in our English translations is "The ancient serpent or serpent of old." The correct interpretation of this Archaios is "original." This serpent gets thrown down in the end times in Revelation 12, not in Genesis.

Again, the Satan as referenced in this verse in Corinthians is a reference to our natures. That deplorable rebellious nature God told us about in Genesis. Paul told the wives to submit to their husbands, so he does not fall victim to his own nature. We are not innocent; we are subjugated to that rebellious nature. The book of Romans tells us a lot about this nature.

If Satan were just a singular entity, even with help from his angels, it still would be logistically impossible for him to inhabit or control billions of people. In fact, Satan and his influence would be diluted as the population grew. That has not happened. The spirit of Satan's influence has grown with the increase in the Earth's population but just not in the way people think. That influence is not from the singular entity. Again, that entity does not get thrown out of Heaven until the end time. What has grown is the opposition to God. That is us.

To continue, we look at what Jesus was really saying to Peter:

"Jesus turned and said to Peter, "Get behind me, Satan! You are a stumbling block to me; you do not have in mind the concerns of God, but merely human concerns." — Matthew 16:23 (NIV)

Was Jesus calling Peter, Satan? Was He telling us Peter was possessed by Satan? No. Jesus was not making a reference to the red man with the pitchfork, that singular entity. This was a reference to Peter's nature. What Peter said to Jesus was not in God's plan; it was Peter exhibiting the same nature spelled out in the above verse in Corinthians and the same nature spelled out in the book of Genesis. Peter said something in opposition to Jesus. This verse was Jesus calling out that opposition. Peter was an apostle, even he was not immune to his fallen nature. Neither was Judas or any of the other apostles. Neither were the disciples, and neither are we. It is a constant battle to not oppose God. It is a constant battle we have to fight daily within our nature. Again, Paul went into great detail in the book of Romans about this battle. The adversary to God, that which opposes God is not external, it's internal. It is our nature.

Next, we will look at one of the most profound exchanges in the Bible. So much information can be gained by understanding what actually happened in the book of Job.

"One day the angels came to present themselves before the LORD, and Satan also came with them. 7 The LORD said to Satan, "Where have you come from?" Satan answered the LORD, "From roaming throughout the earth, going back and forth on it." 8 Then the LORD said to Satan, "Have you considered my servant Job? There is no one on earth like him; he is blameless and upright, a man who fears God and shuns evil." 9 "Does Job fear God for nothing?" Satan replied. 10 "Have you not put a hedge around him and his household and everything he has? You have blessed the work of his hands, so that his flocks and herds are spread throughout the land. 11 But now stretch out your hand and strike everything he has, and he will surely curse you to your face." 12 The LORD said to Satan, "Very well, then, everything he has is in your power, but on the man himself do not lay a finger." Then Satan went out from the presence of the LORD." — Job 1:6-12 (NIV)

Meet Satan. Meet the "Archaios serpent." Here he is. This is the singular entity. We will see him again in Matthew chapter 4 as the singular entity who subjected Jesus to temptation.

He is here in the spiritual realm, not the physical one. Again, remember Revelation 12. Satan does not get thrown out of the spiritual realm until the end time. This will answer many questions about the two "serpents."

This was an incredible exchange Satan had with God. God asked Satan where he came from, and Satan's answer to God was unspeakably disrespectful. It was defiant and filled with hate.

"From going to and fro on the earth, and from walking up and down on it." (English Standard Version)

Satan was not making a reference to himself; he was making a reference to us. We are the ones roaming the Earth; we are the ones walking up and down on the face of it. This was an absolute slam at our Creator. Satan was rubbing our rebellion in God's face. It was a reference to the serpent walking on the planet. Us. We are, were and will be part of Satan's rebellion. We are not innocent. We are guilty of opposing God. We rejected Him. We are here because of it. That is what Satan said to God.

Satan could not have been talking about himself; we would have to twist the hell out of Revelation 12 in order for us not to be the serpent of Genesis 3.

This is another paradox. Satan, the singular entity roaming the Earth. Satan will lose; he knows that. So why is he doing what he is doing? What motivation would Satan have to destroy everyone's marriages, their lives, families, countries and so on? Is hatred of God enough of a motivation? Why wouldn't Satan and his angels just give up? You would think they could negotiate a plea deal with God, don't hurt any more of the humans, don't lead them away from Me to spend eternity in Hell and I'll give you a deal, maybe 5 billion years in Hell instead of eternity. It's better than nothing.

Another paradox. If the established Christian doctrine is correct, then why has God not protected us from Satan the singular entity? It would make no sense if we were innocent victims for God not to protect us from such an entity. If we look at this correctly and realize it is us who rebelled against God, we are the adversaries and we are the ones who opposed God then instantly everything comes into focus.

Again, let's look more closely at the description of Satan:

"You belong to your father, the devil, and you want to carry out your father's desires. He was a murderer from the beginning, not holding to the truth, for there is no truth in him. When he lies, he

speaks his native language, for he is a liar and the father of lies." —
John 8:44 (NIV)

This is a fascinating exchange between Jesus and an institutional church leader. This one exchange will tell us a lot about the embodiment of the rebellion, the one we were born into. These leaders were not "Satan worshipers," at least not in the conventional sense. Yes, they lived in man's truth but they were not "Satanic." In this passage, Jesus tells us where these people live, in the embodiment of the rebellion, the serpent of Genesis 3. They did not belong to God; they lived in their rebellion. Everything they did was in accordance with it. They used the ways of man's religion to gain power over men and garnish influence over them. The lies they lived in were in the ways of the rebellion, lust, greed, power, control and all the other reasons why we rebelled in the first place. In today's IC, our leaders are doing the same thing.

"A murderer from the beginning." Who did the red man with the pitch fork murder in the beginning? Abel? Wasn't that Cain? Yes, it was Cain. The "Archaios" serpent, "the Satan," is the father of the rebellion; that seems to be very clear. Those who do not reconcile with God live in the rebellion and belong to it. That is what Jesus was saying. Satan, the singular entity did not murder Abel. It was Cain's fallen nature which murdered his brother. Our unrepented nature, the nature which belongs to the rebellion of which the "Archaios" serpent is a part of. We either belong to this rebellious nature, or we belong to God. Our salvation through Christ is salvation from that rebellion. Reconciliation with God is from that original rebellion. When Paul, a man reconciled with God said "all things are legal," he was making a reference to his salvation which was from the original sin of the rebellion. It is not what is taught today.

Many other verses in the Bible reference Satan, the dragon, the devil, Lucifer or the serpent. We could go through each one and pull out each one is a reference to the singular entity and as well we could identify which ones are references to our natures. Every mention of the dragon is a mention of us. More accurately put the dragon is a reference to a collective nature controlled by Leviathan through the mechanism of tribalism. We will return to this.

Having an understanding of who God is talking about in the above references will be significantly important when we look at the prophecies in Revelation. Both "Satans" are referenced, us and the singular entity. The Bible also references beasts. In no instance in the Bible does one of those beasts' reference Satan, neither Satan as the individual nor Satan as the embodiment, which would be our nature. Not one time.

One example of this is from Revelation 13:1. We will cover this in another chapter.

Our English translations translates this verse in different ways. In one translation, Apostle John writes, *"The dragon stood on the shore of the sea"* and in another, *"And I saw a beast coming up out of the sea . . ."* (NIV)

Other translations read, "As I stood on the shore of the sea." But John wrote this. Was John the Dragon?

Because today's IC has monstrously taught us incorrectly about the serpent and the dragon there is little answer on how this verse can be translated in such a drastically different way. It would seem to be either the Apostle John or Satan. If we have a correct understanding of this, we will see both will be correct. Apostle John was obviously a man belonging to God, the dragon reference was a reference to where he came from. It was the same rebellion we came from. That spirit of Satan, the serpent in Genesis 3, that embodiment of the rebellion. We all came from it including Apostle John. This reference is not the Satan, the singular entity, but rather Apostle John making a reference to his own nature.

No discussion of Satan would be complete unless we look at a few more scriptures. There are many references to evil spirits and demons. Over the years, there has been much conjecture about the demons Jesus sent into the pigs, and of Satan entering Judas. It may require an entire book to explain these things. For our purpose for now and to go forth at our look at the prophecies in Revelation, just a brief comment on these demons.

They are not Satan the entity or his angels, they cannot be. Again, Satan does not get thrown down until the end days. Those "demons or evil spirits" existed because the Bible tells us about them. They are not Satan the singular entity.

If Satan and his angels were here in the flesh on the planet, God's plan would not work for us. Satan does not have that direct connection with us yet. We are here to live in our rebellion without control or direct communication from either Satan or God. Yes, God does intervene in our lives on this planet at His prerogative, His plan and His glory. Satan does not. God gave him permission in the book of Job for God to prove His point. For His glory not Satan's.

"God is our refuge and strength, an ever-present help in trouble." — *Psalm 46:1 (NIV)*

God is with us while at the same time allowing us to live in our rebellion. The constant direct communication with God does not exist. It can't. Making this false claim is dangerous. It will alienate those not feeling that direct divine communication that people falsely claim. Many believers may question their faith or their salvation because of others claiming this direct communication. It's dangerous because it sets up tribalism and the endless amount of litmus tests which come with it.

The study of the demons and evil spirits is outside the scope of this book but does not in any way disprove the premise that Satan is not here. The Bible tells us he is not.

CHAPTER 5:

The Antichrist

In Matthew 23, Jesus eviscerated the leaders of the institutional church. He called them "snakes and hypocrites." Regardless of what we think of the leadership of those synagogues, nothing has changed. The same dynamic is applicable today as it was then for the same reasons. Human nature has not changed; one man putting himself above another has not changed. Even at the time of the early Christian church, a certain dynamic played out. Apostle John told us of a Christian church leader, Diotrephes. This dynamic is crucial for us to understand the antichrist. More importantly, we will need to see it as the "spirit of antichrist." We will return to this man shortly.

In Matthew 24, Jesus told us many would come in His name, claiming to be messiah and lead many astray. Claiming to be messiah, claiming to speak for God. Today's IC has lost its way and are leading the entire planet astray. It is why they will not and cannot answer even basic questions. It's why they cannot and will not support their own doctrine. It is also why today's institutional doctrine sets up an endless number of paradoxes which appear to have no answer, certainly not from the institutional church.

Many people attend these institutions. There is no doubt that there are believers in each denomination. They know something is not right. The leaders understand this. Many times, they will acknowledge a weakness in the doctrine of others but not their own. When they acknowledge the discomfort of their parishioners, they will mention the doctrine of other institutions but preface their message that they are not like the others. These leaders are telling us God is whispering in their ear but then spew out false doctrine. They hold themselves up. They call themselves Father, Reverend and Rabbi. Jesus spoke to this in Matthew 23. Call no man Father, call no man Rabbi and call no man Teacher.

This warrants conversation. Today's institutional church leaders seem to be in violation of these commandments. These leaders rationalize this by saying they are just titles within the church to delineate responsibilities. They say the titles are not in violation because they abide by the spirit of what Jesus said. This may be the case sometimes, but not always. It would be a stretch to think the catholic hierarchy does not use the titles to put one man above another. How could parishioners confess their sins to another man and get absolution for that sin and not have that priest "above" them? The catholic leadership will spew out their rational for their titles as will many other institutions. When they use their titles to put themselves above other, they are in violation of commandments. Many of them are.

"I will show partiality to no one, nor will I flatter any man, 22 for if I were skilled in flattery, my Maker would soon take me away." — Job 32:21 (NIV)

A great deal of our established religion has failed God's people. In a very specific way. From an understanding of this failure and an understanding of the false doctrine, we will be able to now identify the antichrist.

Before we do, we need to see the false teaching of today's church with regard to the antichrist. We will start by looking at the very false information they have given us on this antichrist, and then we will see what Apostle John actually told us. Then we will identify the antichrist. This will be a major shock and will not be accepted by most. None the less, it is true and will be said.

The general thought, accepted doctrine, tells us of an evil man who will come along in the end days and try to take over the world. He will force everyone to take the "mark" of the beast to buy and sell. Believers will need to reject this mark or be lost. This is all a lie. It will never happen. Much of it is based on the beast of Revelation 13 being this antichrist. It is not. The beast of Revelation 13 is the United States. The chapter itself just describes our political system. Once this is understood, the entire story of the antichrist unravels.

If we remove the false premise of the antichrist and look at all the verses being used to support the false narrative, we can then see what those other verses are telling us, the ones the IC uses incorrectly. Let's start by reading the verses used by the IC to support the false narrative and put the true meaning to them.

Institutional Church Doctrine of Antichrist:

Before we look at the first verse the IC uses to explain the antichrist, let's review a couple of things. Daniel was told by God that the end day prophecies would be sealed up until the end days. Daniel 8:26, 12:4 and 12:9. Our institutional church leaders completely blew these verses off. In their arrogance and self-righteousness, they blew them off. They live in complete violation of them. In these violations, false narratives have been formed which have been passed down for many generations. Writers today have taken the old narratives, refined them, put a little different spin on them and sold us books. They're all false.

The end day prophecies identify many things happening in our current time. The United States is a major component to the end day prophecies. So are many of today's politicians and prominent figures. Barack Obama was the diverse king in Daniel and the three Supreme Court justices leaving the bench under Obama were the three uprooted kings. Donald Trump is referenced multiple times. These are end day prophecies. We are in them.

"He will show no regard for the gods of his ancestors or for the one desired by women, nor will he regard any god, but will exalt himself above them all." — Daniel 11:37 (NIV)

The IC tells us the man in this verse is the "antichrist." It is not true, but this false teaching has led into the false narrative about this mythical man. This man in Daniel is not the antichrist. Not even a little. The IC has gotten this verse completely wrong. This verse is telling us the relationship between Barack Obama and Donald Trump. Let's look carefully at it. We spoke to some of this in *Cursed Above All Cattle*. Barack Obama put himself above the IC when he shoved gay marriage down the throat of a mostly unwilling country. He put himself "above all that is called God" which is the institutional church. When he said they will cling to their guns and their Bibles, it was a direct slam on peoples' beliefs. Apparently traditional beliefs may not be all that important to such a man. He will have no regard for the one desired by women. This reference might be less of a reference to the man desired by women than to a deplorable trait in the female's nature. It's both actually.

What man is desired by women? Actors? Athletes? Famous men? How about rich and powerful men? This passage defines the man Barack Obama has little regard for; it defines who the man is, a rich and powerful man. There is so much hatred for Donald Trump now, it may be hard to see this verse for what it is really telling us. It's really just a description of the category of man "he" (Barack Obama) shows no regard to. This man is Donald Trump. There is no antichrist in this verse. It's a false narrative.

To continue to unravel the false information, the IC is given us on the antichrist we will go to;

"While I was thinking about the horns, there before me was another horn, a little one, which came up among them; and three of the first horns were uprooted before it. This horn had eyes like the eyes of a human being and a mouth that spoke boastfully." —Daniel 7:8 (NIV)

This is a very popular verse used by the IC to describe the antichrist. It's false. The little horn is *not* the antichrist. He is just a person; he was a political leader and now is out of office. We went into great detail in the last book about this man. The IC has added him to the mysterious antichrist narrative. It's completely false. The horns which were uprooted are explained in-depth in the last book as well.

This man is not spoken of in a good light, for good reason. It is my belief that Barack Obama has done more damage to this country than any other president in this country's history. If Obama weaponized the IRS to go after conservatives, which I believe he did, if he weaponized the FBI to go after Trump during his campaign, which I believe he did, it would define him as that lawless man. By putting himself above all that is "called God," he has proven himself to be this boastful man.

The little horn is not the antichrist, nor will scripture support such a false claim.

This next verse is also used by the IC to define the antichrist:

"Don't let anyone deceive you in any way, for that day will not come until the rebellion occurs and the man of lawlessness is revealed, the man doomed to destruction. 4 He will oppose and will exalt himself over everything that is called God or is worshiped, so that he sets himself up in God's temple, proclaiming himself to be God". — 2nd Thessalonians 2:3 (NIV)

Again, *Cursed Above All Cattle* explained this passage in great detail. This prophecy has already happened. The man of lawlessness is not the antichrist. That was an assumption told to us by the same church telling us the Earth was flat, the earth is six thousand years old, the enmity of Genesis 3 is between Christ and Satan and there is an age of accountability. In this verse, there is no mention of the term *antichrist*, and there is no connection to what Apostle John mentioned in his letters. This lawless man is not the antichrist. It is beyond assumption. It is beyond misinterpretation. It is false witness from the institutional church.

The only place in the Bible the antichrist is referenced is in the letters of Apostle John. The only place! The antichrist has been taken massively out of context by our IC. All those verses outside of the letters of Apostle John used by the IC to define this man are false interpretations. We will see why, and it will be extremely bad news for the IC. The Apostle John gave us a very big clue to this "antichrist" when he told us the antichrist will come but many other antichrists have already come. The antichrist to come is the "spirit of antichrist," and it is the same antichrist but in just a much larger magnitude. The IC by its very default has missed the mark on this, in an extraordinary way.

One last verse before we move on to the letters of Apostle John.

"And I stood upon the sand of the sea, and saw a beast rise up out of the sea, having seven heads and ten horns, and upon his horns ten crowns, and upon his heads the name of blasphemy." – Revelation 13:1 (NIV)

The IC has relied heavily on this chapter to define the antichrist and to support their false narrative. The problem is, they cannot support what they say. The beast in Revelation 13, the beast with the ten horns and seven heads and the second beast with the two horns are descriptions of political systems. How could this beast be the antichrist? It is not an individual person. It's a collection of people which does not lend itself to what the IC is telling us. In fact, it blows it out of the water. How is it no one has called them out on this lie? If they say the antichrist leads this entity, this beast, keep in mind, there is not one word in the Bible which supports this premise. It is of course, false. The antichrist has no relevance to Revelation 13. It is at its core false doctrine, one in which much doctrine has been based. The understanding of this alone will unravel the myth of this antichrist being a man.

The antichrist in the letters of Apostle John is not referenced in Revelation 13. It is a false doctrine.

What John told is about the antichrist

In the third letter of John, the Apostle told us of a man, Diotrephes. This man was the leader of a church, a Christian church. Apostle John didn't have much good to say about this IC Christian leader.

"I wrote to the church, but Diotrephes, who loves to be first, will not welcome us. (10) So when I come, I will call attention to what he is doing, spreading malicious nonsense about us. Not satisfied with that, he even refuses to welcome other believers. He also stops

those who want to do so and puts them out of the church." — 3 John 1:9 (NIV)

Read about this "Christian leader"; he puts "himself first"; he puts believers out of his church, and he spreads nonsense about someone chosen by God. Is today any different than two thousand years ago? How many Diotrephes's are there out there right now teaching the church? They are putting themselves above others; they call themselves Father and Rabbi. Have you ever noticed that you never hear of Diotrephes in church or Bible study? Jesus was critical on the institutional church leaders. Apostle John was critical of this institutional Christian church leader. Today's IC will not have that; they will not tolerate criticism even from John. Todays' church is the Laodicea church. The majority of churches today are being led by Diotrephes. They call themselves "Father," "Rabbi" and "Reverend." They put themselves over their parishioners. Jesus told them not to do this. Today's IC leaders are in violation of the commandments of Jesus if they use their titles to elevate themselves over their parishioners. They are promulgating massive false doctrine for their own good and not for the glory of God but for their own glory. It's why they cannot admit to teaching things they now know to be fundamentally wrong, like the age of the Earth. If they were to admit error for that false teaching, it would show that they do not have the preponderance of the truth as they claim and as Diotrephes no doubt claimed. The doctrine of the Earth being young has generated many other false doctrines which would need to be corrected. Today's Laodicea church, the ones being run by the Diotrephes's on this planet, will not allow a shift to the truth to happen. It would require changes to even basic doctrine like the creation story itself. They will not change in the same way the Scribes and Pharisees would not change from their false doctrine. They are opposing God at the same time they claim to be advocating for God. They are the ones saying "Lord, Lord." Jesus told us this would happen. He warned us!

Before we go on with this, we need to repeat something. God's people live in every denomination. The body of Christ are the people who belong to God. We are saved by grace and faith, not knowledge. If we understand this, then we can get a clear understanding of the seven churches in Revelation. They worshiped differently, had different doctrines and yet walked in faith with God. The churches differed but still belonged to God. Faith and grace, not knowledge, will put meaning to Romans 3:11, "no one seeks God, no one understands" (NIV). If our knowledge was required, we would all be lost. We will speak about the seven churches in the next chapter. We will also speak about and put meaning to the two-sided scroll of Revelation 5 which is relevant to this conversation. The body of Christ sits in the pews but not necessarily stands at the pulpit. What Jesus said in Matthew 23 still applies today.

John told us:

"Dear children, this is the last hour; and as you have heard that the antichrist is coming, even now many antichrists have come. This is how we know it is the last hour. 19 They went out from us, but they did not really belong to us. For if they had belonged to us, they would have remained with us; but their going showed that none of them belonged to us." — 1 John 2:18 (NIV)

This passage, seen in the correct context, unlocks the identity of the antichrist. "as you have heard." Yes, they did hear from Christ Himself and no other. All those other verses the IC uses to define the antichrist are false. The only mention of the antichrist is here in the letters of Apostle John and what Christ said in Matthew 24:

5 "For many will come in my name, claiming, 'I am the Messiah,' and will deceive many."

23 "At that time if anyone says to you, 'Look, here is the Messiah!' or, 'There he is!' do not believe it."

24 "For false messiahs and false prophets will appear and perform great signs and wonders to deceive, if possible, even the elect." (NIV)

These three verses may be the most important verses for our current time. They will also identify the antichrist. "claiming to be messiah" (claiming to speak for God) "here is the Messiah" (someone claiming to have that direct two-way communication with God) and "deceive, if possible, even the elect" (deceive the body of Christ). Our institutional church leaders are lying to us. They are claiming a relationship with God they do not have. If the prophet Balaam did not have the constant direct communication with God (the scripture tells us he went against God), how would the men of great status today have what he did not? Our mega church leaders, the men on the "circuit" doing seminars for a hefty price, on whose behalf are they acting? If it were for the glory of God, they would not say the things they do. Or live the way they live. They would not accept deference, nor would they exalt themselves above others as they all do, as Diotrephes did.

In Apostle John's letters, he speaks of that false leader Diotrephes. In the same letters, he tells us of the antichrist, the only place it is mentioned in the Bible.

Today's Christian churches are the churches of Diotrephes. Today's institutional church is spreading false doctrine and lying to us about God. The "many would come in my name" have to themselves to be Christian churches, or they could not come in "his name." The many does not mean the few. It means many.

"Who is a liar but he that denieth that Jesus is the Christ? He is antichrist, that denieth the Father and the Son." —1 John 2:22 (NIV)

As Diotrephes put himself first, so do most all of today's IC leaders, and they are spreading misinformation about God as Diotrephes did.

Today's established Christian doctrine tell us we are born innocent until we reach the age of accountability. This false doctrine tells us we personally pay for the sin of Adam and Eve. That the enmity of Genesis 3 was between Christ and Satan. These are all lies. If this doctrine is true, then God would be a heartless unloving cruel God. He would be indifferent to our suffering and pain.

Yes, Adam and Eve brought sin into the world, but we do not pay for their sin; we pay for our own. That sin that happened before the foundation of the world. The sin of rebelling against God. Today's church does not tell us this.

Christ sacrificed for us because of us. In the above false doctrine, Christ sacrificed for us because of someone else's rebellion which denies our guilt and negates salvation through Christ. Today's institutional church denies our rebellion of God took place before the foundation of the Earth. This changes the character of God from a loving God to an evil God, thus denying God's character and why Christ died for us. This has to be true. No one affiliated with the Christian religion would follow someone denying Jesus was the Christ. Not one. If they were not affiliated with the Christian religion, what difference would it make who they followed? The institutional church is lying to us to cover themselves. To cover for their false doctrines. This is those who *"denieth that Jesus is the Christ."*

Today's Christian institutional church is the spirit of antichrist. The antichrist is not a person; it's a spirit of antichrist. Those who deny the true reason Christ died for us. To see this truth, we will need to shift from our current understanding of salvation. Shift from believing that Christ just died for us to believing Christ died because of us. The spirit of antichrist makes our Creator a cruel and heartless God. It erases the sacrifice of Jesus. That is what John was telling us. The mystery man is a fable. He does not exist.

"They are from the world and therefore speak from the viewpoint of the world, and the world listens to them. 6 We are from God, and whoever knows God listens to us; but whoever is not from God does not listen to us. This is how we recognize the Spirit of truth and the spirit of falsehood." —1 John 4:5

This is extremely relevant today. "The world listens to them." We have many well-known respected church leaders today. Some very popular authors have written books read by millions. They sell out before they are even published sometimes. These men are loved by millions. How does that square with this passage? These books, they seem to be given us what we seek. But do they really do this? Most of the books and the sermons we read and hear refine old established narratives with slightly different spin. They give us no specific information on the prophecies, and they don't mention our rebellion. These are the leaders who "tickle their ears" and spread myths and fables against God. By doing this, they deny the Christ.

We are in a world full of Diotrephes. The world listens to them. This is the antichrist.

CHAPTER 6:

The Seven Churches

Above the obscuration, above the mystery, the prophecies in the book of Revelation can be understood. From this knowledge, the number of the beast was calculated. The beasts were identified, and the massive corruption of our institutional church has been exposed.

In this chapter, we will look at the seven churches in the book of Revelation. They tell us a lot about who we are. Although it may seem impossible to categorize today's current religious organizations because of the apparent vast differences between them, they all have the same characteristic which will put them in similarity to one of these seven churches. There are vast differences within our denominations on social issues, but the differences don't end there. There are also differences in the way the denominations worship, certainly comparing a Catholic service with a Southern Baptist service, the difference would be stark. On the surface, it looks like the seven churches follow suit, with differences in the way worship is done and the way its doctrine is taught. But this is where the similarities end.

All churches today follow a similar if not exact doctrine, a blue-print of sorts. From a casual observation, it looks as though today's denominations are drastically different. This is surface level only. If we look deeper down, we will see a common thread in an established doctrine. Much deeper than the differences on social issues. Yes, there are drastic differences on gay marriage, abortion and many other social issues. We think these are substantial issues and support our belief or justify it by our interpretation of the scriptures.

If we dig deeper, we will see the commonality in established doctrine; it is in this commonality which puts our current institutional churches in the Laodicea church. In chapter 20 of this book, I devote an entire chapter to comparing man's truth with what is actually in the Bible. Our entire religious establishment has gone astray because of it.

In the established doctrine, the entity of Satan is taught the same way. In past generations, the entity of Satan has been taught drastically different than it is taught today, it was taught as the "spirit of Satan" and not as the entity. Today, the established doctrine of Satan is completely false as was spelled out in a previous chapter. Established doctrine also has the enmity in Genesis 3 being between Christ and Satan and not being between male and female. This is false doctrine but it is "accepted doctrine".

These false doctrines have made God and God's words into fables. They have made man innocent victims of those who came before us. Their entire premise of who we are has been missed in today's institutions. That is the lukewarm church; that is the Laodicea church. Our churches have made God and Jesus euphemisms. People have been lulled to sleep.

We will go through each of the seven churches in the book of Revelation. They differ in doctrine, in the way they worship and in the weaknesses they have within them. But they all belong to God or at least have a path back.

Church of Ephesus

"To the angel of the church in Ephesus write: These are the words of him who holds the seven stars in his right hand and walks among the seven golden lampstands. 2 I know your deeds, your hard work and your perseverance. I know that you cannot tolerate wicked people, that you have tested those who claim to be apostles but are not, and have found them false." — Revelation 2:1 (NIV)

Something positive is said here. Those who belong to God live in this church. They are the true believers, the ones reconciled with God. We make the assumption that the one who walks among the lampstand is Jesus and that He acknowledges those who belong to Him are in this church.

"You have persevered and have endured hardships for my name, and have not grown weary. 4 Yet I hold this against you: You have forsaken the love you had at first. 5 Consider how far you have fallen! Repent and do the things you did at first. If you do not repent, I will come to you and remove your lampstand from its place." — **Revelation 2:3 (NIV)**

They persevered, a good thing, but they lost their fire, a bad thing. There are many ways a church can backslide, lose fire and get tired. Jesus wasn't happy about this and warned them.

"But you have this in your favor: You hate the practices of the Nicolaitans, which I also hate." — Revelation 2:6 (NIV)

"Whoever has ears, let them hear what the Spirit says to the churches. To the one who is victorious, I will give the right to eat

from the tree of life, which is in the paradise of God." —Revelation 2:7 (NIV)

Little seems to be known about what the Nicolaitans did, but they seemed to be in conformance to the Roman political system idolatry. A ritualistic worship. I assume this to be the origin of the Catholic Church. Jesus hated what the Nicolaitans did. He told us this. They fell away from the faith and substituted it for their own rituals.

There are important concepts about this church of Ephesus which need to be understood. They had flaws, and they weren't perfect, but they belonged to God. This is very significant. Today's institutional church does not appear to believe they have flaws. They say things like they have "commonality of the spirit" or "our doctrine is perfect, but it's our knowledge that is incomplete." It's arrogant. This church had flaws and they were victims of tribalism, but they belonged to God. And this is an early church. The interesting thing about this church will be when we see the church of Pergamum. They did adhere to the teaching of the Nicolaitans. This is an important point. Jesus said He hated that but the church of Pergamum had His people in it. Curious. They had different doctrine and worshiped differently but still belonged to God. We will give the meaning to this later in the book when we describe the two-sided scroll. It will be extraordinarily important to understand the two-sided scroll.

Another very important concept. The first six churches were praised and criticized. They had the body of Christ, believers in them. The seventh was not praised. It was warned. Best to heed that warning.

Church of Smyrna

"To the angel of the church in Smyrna write: These are the words of him who is the First and the Last, who died and came to life again. 9 I know your afflictions and your poverty—yet you are rich! I know about the slander of those who say they are Jews and are not, but are a synagogue of Satan."—Revelation 2:8 (NIV)

If Satan and his angels don't get thrown out of Heaven until later on in Revelation, in the end days, who is this Satan? Not the one from Genesis 3; that was us. In the book of Job, Satan shows up with the angels. He tells God he goes "to and fro" on the planet. Satan was talking about us; we are the ones going "to and fro" on the planet. Satan was disrespectful to God. We are the rebellion. If they were the "synagogue of Satan," they do not belong to God; they belonged to their nature. John 8:44, their father Satan. That Satan is the nature of the rebellion. Our nature. That's what this verse is telling us.

When Herod ordered the killing of all those babies, he didn't have his men go to the house of baby Jesus and kill Him. In fact, he didn't know who He was. Herod killed all of the children the approximate age of Jesus. If it was being driven by Satan the entity, the devil, killing all the two-year-olds would not have been necessary. The "Satan" that tried to kill Him was man, our nature, the rebellion. They were the spirit of Satan, not Satan the entity for who they were not linked to nor have direct contact with. The entity of Satan does not have that authority. When Herod had the babies killed, Satan had not been thrown out of Heaven yet. Two different references to Satan. Satan the entity and one the spirit of Satan which is our nature, the embodiment of the rebellion.

We are no more linked to the entity of Satan, the devil, the original serpent than we are with God. It has to be this way, or there would be no purpose for us being on this planet. We are allowed to live in our rebellion without the direct influence of God or Satan the entity. It is extraordinarily important to understand this. It has to be the case. Satan would not have tried to kill Jesus; he could not have. He knew this. He knew he would not have the authority to ever even attempt such a thing. The death of Jesus came from our rebellion. Our nature, that spirit of Satan.

The description of these churches proves that they lack "commonality of the spirit." That is not required to reconcile with God. We would all be lost if that were the case and only one of these churches would belong to God. If that were the case only one of todays' denominations would belong to God.

"Do not be afraid of what you are about to suffer. I tell you; the devil will put some of you in prison to test you, and you will suffer persecution for ten days." — Revelation 2:10 (NIV)

The devil is not here yet. The devil in this verse are those who have not reconciled with God. We are most certainly not innocent. This church is under the mystery. They think they have the preponderance of the truth. They do not, none of us do. They have no idea why they are on the planet. No idea that we were the serpent. No idea Satan the entity will not arrive until the end days. The evil on this planet comes from us, the embodiment of the rebellion against God. Satan and God are bystanders in what is happening on this planet. All the while Satan accuses God's people day and night. The Bible tells us this. We have this all wrong. Yes, God maintains authority to intervene in our lives and He does answer prayer. God maintains control over this planet to the extent necessary to ensure the process remains in place. That control will not stop the pain we cause nor will it intervene on the man-made consequences which happen as a function of our rebellion. If this were the case, than all of those past evil dictators we have had on this planet would have been stuck down by God. The van full of kids would not crash, and the tornado would not hit a church. God maintains control to keep the process in place, not to intervene in the consequences of man. Saying so is a lie. He is letting us live in our rebellion for which we pay for those consequences. God does not have the direct communication with us as our institutional church leaders tell us. They say things like "the lord spoke to my heart" or "the spirit led me," but remember what Jesus told us about this, "claiming to be messiah," that is claiming to speak for God. They are lying to us or to themselves and leading people astray. God chooses who He communicates with, and it is never for the glory of man. When our church leaders allude to this direct communication, it is for their own glory. It works for increasing their status or for commercial gain, but they kill the truth when they do such things. All the while God has allowed us to live in this rebellion. If this were not the case, God would have stopped this planet long ago.

"Be faithful, even to the point of death, and I will give you life as your victor's crown. 11 Whoever has ears, let them hear what the Spirit says to the churches. The one who is victorious will not be hurt at all by the second death." (NIV)

The Spirit is saying they are under the mystery. The truth does not belong to them. They are reconciled with God, but they do not own the truth. We have all rebelled against God. We are told to put no man above another, call no man Rabbi. Where is the "commonality of the spirit" on this? The churches are different from one another, and yet they are reconciled with God. Knowledge is not required, only faith.

"For it is by grace you have been saved, through faith . . ."—Ephesians 2:8 (NIV)

Church of Pergamum

"I know where you live—where Satan has his throne. Yet you remain true to my name. You did not renounce your faith in me, not even in the days of Antipas, my faithful witness, who was put to death in your city—where Satan lives." —Revelation 2:13 (NIV)

Again, this Satan is not the Archaios serpent, the devil, Lucifer; that entity is not on the Earth yet. Satan and his angels are in Heaven and have not been thrown out yet. He has no spiritual link to us. We are this Satan; it is our nature of rebellion. The big point here is "you remain true." The importance of this will be to dispel comments such as "commonality of the spirit" and "God didn't tell me, therefore what you say is not true." There is no link, at least not in the way we have been told, neither to the Archaios serpent nor to God.

"Nevertheless, I have a few things against you: There are some among you who hold to the teaching of Balaam, who taught Balak to entice the Israelites to sin so that they ate food sacrificed to idols and committed sexual immorality." —Revelation 2:14 (NIV)

The rules for sexual morality are set forth in Leviticus 18 and not the sexual immorality the institutional church has taught us from implying it from some scripture but ignoring others. The doctrine of man is so far off. So much church doctrine has little to no support in the scripture. They justify it by claiming a knowledge beyond the scripture and prove its truth in "accepted doctrine through commonality of the spirit" which is man's truth, not God's truth. It's still important to understand they still belonged to God. This church had in it sexual immorality, something in which todays church considers the ultimate unrighteousness. But they were praised and criticized. The body of Christ lived in this church.

"Likewise, you also have those who hold to the teaching of the Nicolaitans. 16 Repent therefore! Otherwise, I will soon come to

you and will fight against them with the sword of my mouth. 17 Whoever has ears, let them hear what the Spirit says to the churches. To the one who is victorious, I will give some of the hidden manna. I will also give that person a white stone with a new name written on it, known only to the one who receives it."—Revelation 2:15 (NIV)

Again, the secret to the letters to the churches is in the two-sided scroll. These churches are on one side (which is man's side), that is under the mystery. This is why we are told to put no man above another. It's why we have not figured out the prophecies. It's why there is so much difference between the denominations, and it's why "no one understands, no one seeks God" which, as it turns out, is an important verse. We don't need to understand to reconcile. We reconcile by faith only. God's truth is on the other side of the scroll, above the mystery. The truth of who we really are will not be found until the mystery is lifted. The mystery of why we are here.

They worshiped in a way Jesus said He hated, but still, the body of Christ lived in this church.

Church of Thyatira

"To the angel of the church in Thyatira write: These are the words of the Son of God, whose eyes are like blazing fire and whose feet are like burnished bronze."—Revelation 2:18 (NIV)

It's interesting that the description of Christ is different for each church.

"I know your deeds, your love and faith, your service and perseverance, and that you are now doing more than you did at first."—Revelation 2:19 (NIV)

A good comment. The members of this church belonged to God, and they walked in faith. They were reconciled with God. Then Jesus mentioned they are doing something wrong.

"Nevertheless, I have this against you: You tolerate that woman Jezebel, who calls herself a prophet. By her teaching she misleads my servants into sexual immorality and the eating of food sacrificed to idols. 21 I have given her time to repent of her immorality, but she is unwilling. 22 So I will cast her on a bed of suffering, and I will make those who commit adultery with her suffer intensely, unless they repent of her ways. 23 I will strike her children dead. Then all the churches will know that I am he who searches hearts and minds, and I will repay each of you according to your deeds." — Revelation 2:20 (NIV)

Jesus acknowledges they are reconciled, then says this, they are being sexually immoral. Led by this female Jezebel. These believers are not living in accordance with the commandments, but they are reconciled. They will be punished.

"Now I say to the rest of you in Thyatira, to you who do not hold to her teaching and have not learned Satan's so-called deep secrets, 'I will not impose any other burden on you, 25 except to hold on to what you have until I come.'" — Revelation 2:24 (NIV)

Not everyone in this church was on board with what Jezebel was teaching. It was of a sexual nature. "Satan's so-called secrets" were again, not the devil, Lucifer or the singular entity. This is a reference to our sexual nature. The "secret" may not be much of a secret today. It alludes to a conversation that will never be had in our churches or Bible studies today. Jezebel had apparently been teaching members how to reduce their sexual inhibitions. All of which were outside the bounds of morality, sexual activity not condoned by God. Most people will have no idea about this. Those who council couples or do sexual therapy may have a better under-standing. There are many things couples experiment with sexually to increase libido or otherwise increase the intensity of the couple's sex life. As uncomfortable as it is to talk about, stifling conversa-tion on such things really hides the truth. Not all of it is moral in the eyes of our Creator. The phrase "Satan's secret" is incredibly important to understand. It's a comment about our sexual nature, not about the devil. This sexual statement is made here in this pas-sage and therefore should not avoided. It is often avoided by the IC because they are uncomfortable with it, as they are uncomfortable speaking about our natures. Many people may go their entire lives and never understand some of the things in our sexual nature. The institutional church seldom broaches these topics, and when they do, it is at a very shallow and superficial level. Basic functions of our biological natures are not discussed because they feel it inap-propriate or are embarrassed by such things. The Bible has no such restriction as it is a man-made restriction. The sexual libido can be driven to a very high level. To achieve this, some amount of sexual inhibitions needs to be overcome. This is what Jezebel was doing; she understood how to lower the sexual inhibitions, thus, knew how to increase the sexual intensity. Apparently, she achieved this by being in violation of Gods' commandments. She was female with few cultural or moral restrictions. All the conversation sur-rounding this are stifled by today's institutional church, like a wet blanket covering the truth because it would require uncomfortable conversations on topics never spoken of in church, Bible studies or maybe in polite conversation. "So-called secret" is not a secret, a mystery or magical. It's embedded in our nature.

When our sexual natures are spoken of by the IC, which is seldom, none of the multitude of negative references to the female nature are made. In the previous book, we identified the difference in the male and female nature as the enmity God put between us. That knowledge led to the identification of the serpent in Genesis and thus broke open the prophecies. All from a topic which is never broached in church. Maybe the leaders think it inappropriate or irrelevant. Our basic nature irrelevant.

The leaders will never speak to all the negative descriptions of the female nature throughout the entire Bible. Those scriptures are off limits. No doubt they do not wish to anger half their demographics. So, the truth stays hidden and the leaders keep everyone happy. Those descriptions are not driven by culture but by nature which has not changed. They still apply.

26 "To the one who is victorious and does my will to the end, I will give authority over the nations—27 that one 'will rule them with an iron scepter and will dash them to pieces like pottery'—just as I have received authority from my Father. 28 I will also give that one the morning star. 29 Whoever has ears, let them hear what the Spirit says to the churches." (NIV)

The common theme we see with this church as with the others is the lack of "commonality of the spirit." These people are saved and walking in faith. Sexual immorality made its way into this church, but they were different than the others. They were under the mystery, the obscuration. They were reconciled through faith, not knowledge or works. If that were not the case, they would be lost as would the rest of us.

Church of Sardis

"To the angel of the church in Sardis write: These are the words of him who holds the seven spirits of God and the seven stars. I know your deeds; you have a reputation of being alive, but you are dead. 2 Wake up! Strengthen what remains and is about to die, for I have

found your deeds unfinished in the sight of my God." — Revelation 3:1 (NIV)

There is very significant language in this passage. "Reputation of being alive, but you are dead." How many of these churches do we know today! They are grandiose and have audiences of thousands. They play music, shout about prosperity and spew out euphemisms about God. They speak in a very shallow superficial level on the scriptures. Don't mention anything politically incorrect, and don't hold their members accountable. Placate them, tickle their ears and make the Word into myths and fables. Tell people how great they are and how they too can be prosperous. Everyone feels good; the service is lively; we have a reputation of being alive and vibrant, and they have many devout members. But they are dead but still are in a church. Believers live in this dead place. Knowledge is not required for salvation, only faith.

The reconciliation of members should not be questioned but their knowledge should be.

"Remember, therefore, what you have received and heard; hold it fast, and repent. But if you do not wake up, I will come like a thief, and you will not know at what time I will come to you. 4 Yet you have a few people in Sardis who have not soiled their clothes. They will walk with me, dressed in white, for they are worthy." — Revelation 3:3 (NIV).

Even in this awful place, the reconciled lived. "Yet you have a few." Even horrible church buildings have people who belong to God.

"The one who is victorious will, like them, be dressed in white. I will never blot out the name of that person from the book of life, but will acknowledge that name before my Father and his angels.

6 Whoever has ears, let them hear what the Spirit says to the churches." — *Revelation 3:5 (NIV)*

Church of Philadelphia

"To the angel of the church in Philadelphia write: These are the words of him who is holy and true, who holds the key of David. What he opens no one can shut, and what he shuts no one can open. 8 I know your deeds. See, I have placed before you an open door that no one can shut. I know that you have little strength, yet you have kept my word and have not denied my name." — *Revelation 3:7 (NIV)*

"Have little strength." Not likely a reference to spiritual strength but maybe one of influence. Unlike the church with the reputation of "being alive," this church is low key and some of its members are believers. They hold fast to their faith and abide by the commandments. This is a good church to be a member of. Jesus told us this church had not "denied my name". In the true look at the antichrist spirit, we saw churches which did deny Christ by holding themselves up as innocent; this church did not. By denying that we are responsible for our own rebellion, we deny that Christ died because of us. If we blame Adam and Eve, it makes us innocent victims and makes God to be something He is not. By denying our rebellion, we are Gods' fault and not responsible for our own rebellion. That is what this church did not do; that was not their doctrine. That's today's institutional church's doctrine.

"I will make those who are of the synagogue of Satan, who claim to be Jews though they are not, but are liars—I will make them come and fall down at your feet and acknowledge that I have loved you." — *Revelation 3:9 (NIV)*

Jesus knew who they belonged to. Not the "devil", the singular entity. This Satan, again, was a reference that these men belonged to their nature. They worshiped in man's truth, and they belonged to their father, Satan (John 8:44). They belonged to their nature of the rebellion. They did not belong to God; they belonged to man.

"Since you have kept my command to endure patiently, I will also keep you from the hour of trial that is going to come on the whole world to test the inhabitants of the earth." — Revelation 3:10 (NIV)

This church and those in it who belong to God will not go through the end day trials. We know this because we are told it. We will not be so fortunate. Those alive today are not members of this church.

"I am coming soon. Hold on to what you have, so that no one will take your crown. 12 The one who is victorious I will make a pillar in the temple of my God. Never again will they leave it. I will write on them the name of my God and the name of the city of my God, the new Jerusalem, which is coming down out of heaven from my God; and I will also write on them my new name. 13 Whoever has ears, let them hear what the Spirit says to the churches." — Revelation 3: 11 (NIV)

This church was praised. The body of Christ lived in this church.

Church of Laodicea

"To the angel of the church in Laodicea write: These are the words of the Amen, the faithful and true witness, the ruler of God's creation." (NIV)

Revelation 3:15 "I know your deeds, that you are neither cold nor hot. I wish you were either one or the other! 16 So, because you are lukewarm — neither hot nor cold — I am about to spit you out of my mouth." — Revelation 3:14 (NIV)

Not hot or cold, this is where the deceit lies. This is today's church, neither hot nor cold. They are keeping their parishioners in the dark. They tickle their ears and spread myths about God. They keep them comfortable in their ignorance of God and of us. They say we are born into the sin of Adam and Eve making us innocent and God guilty of bringing us into this world. Into a threat of eternal damnation if we don't reconcile with a God who isn't readily apparent. In this world, we're basically good but God is mean, unloving and unjust. That is not what they say with their words; after all, they constantly tell us of God's love and constantly spew out euphemisms about the death of Christ. But what are they really saying? We need to reconcile with God through Christ because we are innocent victims born into a sinful world through no fault of our own? That is the denial of Christ. Today's institutional church "sells" us salvation. In their salvation story, they are the ones who give it to you. They give you little true knowledge of scripture. They give you no knowledge of our rebellion. They twist scripture in a way that gives them power and authority as the scribes and the pharisees did. They glorify themselves. They sell a guilt free life in which its members can pursue their "motivations of the fall" and live without fear of accountability. Say the salvation prayer and you are covered. Go forth and pursue your idols. This Laodicean church is extremely dangerous to those who belong to God.

"You say, 'I am rich; I have acquired wealth and do not need a thing.' But you do not realize that you are wretched, pitiful, poor, blind and naked" — *Revelation 3:17 (NIV).*

These are the words of today's institutional church. They say "our doctrine is perfect; it's our knowledge which is incomplete." They say Jesus whispers in their ears then claim to speak for Him. They say "we have a commonality in the spirit and speak one message from the Bible." Therefore, established doctrine is not to be questioned or strayed from. Don't violate the rules of the tribe, "belong to one of our institutions or you will have no credibility and will not to be listened to." And yet this lukewarm church won't answer questions about why we are here. That "questions the solvency of God" they say. That is false. These questions question the wisdom of man; it questions the doctrine of man. Today's institutional church doctrine sets up paradoxes which can't be answered because questions can't be asked. Like abortion, it sounds like a wonderful thing, killing an unborn baby covered by this "age of accountability." After all, we would be sentencing our children to spend eternity with God. Would not abortion be a wonderful thing? After all, it is the law of the land. Or the paradox of a young teenager who dies unreconciled and spends eternity in Hell? Seems like a disproportionate punishment, doesn't it? Infinitely disproportionate. Another paradox which can't be answered by the Laodicea church. Subjects that cannot be broached. This is our current church. It is blind.

"I counsel you to buy from me gold refined in the fire, so you can become rich; and white clothes to wear, so you can cover your shameful nakedness; and salve to put on your eyes, so you can see. 19 Those whom I love I rebuke and discipline. So be earnest and repent. 20 Here I am! I stand at the door and knock. If anyone hears my voice and opens the door, I will come in and eat with that person, and they with me." — Revelation 3:18 (NIV)

It's crystal clear, Jesus wants us to reconcile. Even in this church, which is teaching a doctrine preventing us from seeing the love of God.

"To the one who is victorious, I will give the right to sit with me on my throne, just as I was victorious and sat down with my Father on his throne. 22 Whoever has ears, let them hear what the Spirit says to the churches." — Revelation 3:21 (NIV)

These churches tell us something. For many years, it was difficult to understand why the description of these churches was placed here in the book of Revelation. It now can be understood, and it will not be good for today's institutional church.

In today's church buildings, it seems as though many if not all do a similar thing. They allude to a common theme; the truth lives here in this church but the other churches have lost their way. "Their stance on social issues is wrong" or their ritualism is wrong or even their doctrine is off. Come to our church; it's not in darkness, and we have the light of truth here.

This mentality, this mantra conflicts with what the Bible is telling us about the seven churches. They had different ways in which they worshiped, and they had different doctrines. Tribalism had worked its way into the church, but they still belonged to God. Ritualistic worship which Jesus hated, and he criticized it but did not condemn the church that did it. Jesus condemned sexual immorality, but again, he did not condemn the church. When we understand about the scroll with the writing on both sides in Revelation chapter 5, we will understand why there are such differences in our doctrines and yet we belong to the same God. The Laodicea church was not even condemned; they were given a path back to God.

We are in this church today. It's why we have never seen or understood the prophesies. It's why they tell us we are born innocent. It's why they think established doctrine is not "man's truth but God's truth." It's why they claim God whispers in their ears but then spew out that which is under the mystery. What message do we get in today's church?

Over and over again, the story of salvation. Jesus died for us; Jesus died for us. Is there a single one of the 2.18 billion people claiming to be Christians not knowing that message? Why is the central theme and almost the only theme at church a singular message? Jesus died for us; Jesus died for us, but that in its entirety is not the full truth. It's in the incompleteness of this truth in which the denial of Christ lives. Jesus did not just die for us; he died for us because of us. We all own a part of it. We are not innocent. We are guilty. He died because of us. Everyone on this Earth, everyone who has ever lived owns a part of His death. He died because we rebelled against God before the foundation of the planet. We are here because of it. We are not innocent victims.

We need to listen. The first six churches were praised or praised and criticized. The body of Christ, the invisible church, the remnant lived in those churches. They belonged to God even though they had less than perfect worship and less than pure righteousness. They worshiped in a way in which God said He hated and had sexual immorality in it but were praised and criticized. The seventh church was not praised and criticized. It was rebuked and defined as lukewarm. Even that church was offered a way back. Today's Laodicean church needs to change its ways. They need to leave this doctrine which hides God's character and hides our rebellion. Or they will be spewed out of the mouth of God.

The warning has been given.

CHAPTER 7

The Two-Sided Scroll

"Then I saw in the right hand of him who sat on the throne a scroll with writing on both sides and sealed with seven seals." — *Revelation 5:1 (NIV)*

This may be one of the most important verses in the entire Bible. The knowledge of this will explode open all the prophecies. It will answer so many questions. An understanding of this two-sided scroll will reveal the mystery.

The two-sided scroll is a great dichotomy between man and God. On one side of the scroll is man; it's us under the obscuration. The other side of the scroll is God. God's truth, the correct story of who we are and why God created us.

"But you, Daniel, close up and seal the words of the scroll until the time of the end. Many will go here and there to increase knowledge." — *Daniel 12:4 (NIV)*

There is a great deal of information available to us in this verse. In a previous chapter, we looked at the seven churches. There was an interesting fact about them which has not been addressed by today's IC. They had different doctrines and worshiped differently, but they still belonged to God. This is very telling about this two-sided scroll. Man's truth is not God's truth. Man has been drastically wrong from the beginning. Man has lived in his rebellion from the beginning. This was the plan from the beginning. Those who belong to God are not required to affiliate with a particular denomination or any specific worship. If that were true, then the ritualistic worship of the Catholic Church members would disqualify them from salvation, as it would have of the church of Pergamum who adhered to the practices of the Nicolaitans. Something Jesus told us He hated, in fact He commended Church of Ephesus for not adhering with those practices. This is a conversation the institutional church will never have. For a multitude of reasons. Not the least of which is that no organized religion will admit they live with incomplete doctrine which is our side of the scroll. The IC will have us believe they live on God's side and therefore have the "preponderance" of the truth. That is the arrogance of man as transmitted by the men that put themselves over one another, the IC leaders. That is why Jesus excoriated them in Matthew 23. Nothing has changed. The nature of man has not changed, and our church leaders today do not understand they are living in the man's side of the scroll. If this were not the case, there would only be one denomination. Only one denomination would have the truth. This is not the case. This is why we do not put one man over another. That was a commandment Jesus gave us. Reconciling with God through Christ requires faith and repentance and not knowledge of the other side of the scroll. We may never have that knowledge on this planet. We will have the knowledge that the dichotomy exists. That is what this verse is telling us.

Men think they have the answer. They think they have the truth. Man will always fall short on our side of the scroll.

The leaders of our churches today will not acknowledge this. They put themselves above others. They tell us they speak for God. They do not. They dress up in fancy garments during church service and perform ritualistic worship. They accept deference and hold themselves up. Jesus told them not to do this. All of us fall short, even our leaders, especially the leaders telling us they speak for God. They speak to our side of the scroll but will not acknowledge what Christ told us.

We all fall drastically short. We all rebelled against God. We all live here in our rebellion because of it. We live on our side of the scroll.

There are drastic doctrinal differences between denominations as well as differences within the same denominations. We have drastic differences between churches on social issues. Each church thinking it has the preponderance of the truth, the truth "lives with them" in their church and in their denominations. They don't understand, we are all living in our rebellion on our side of the scroll and will always fall short because of it. Again, it is what the descriptions of the seven churches was telling us.

The Bible told us something;

"There is no one who understands; there is no one who seeks God." — Romans 3:11 (NIV)

The institutional church has twisted the hell out of this verse because they don't understand it. They say, "No this is not us, we seek God, we do understand, it's the folks in those other churches that don't. The truth lives with us, in our church and in our doctrine. This verse does not apply to us."

As long as we do not acknowledge why we are here on this planet, we will always live in this verse. Since those who belong to Jesus do reconcile with God, it does not mean they have the knowledge of the scroll. They reconcile with repentance and faith not knowledge. If this were the case, this verse would have never been written. If knowledge of this scroll was required, we would not have differences in our denominations, and the book of Revelation would not have given us a description of the seven churches. If knowledge was required none of us would reconcile.

Let's look closely at this two-sided scroll. It has two different narratives: one is above the obscuration, and the other is under the obscuration. Two different premises. If we understand the difference, everything makes sense, and we will understand what the two-sided scroll is.

Under the obscuration (under the mystery) which is on man's side of the scroll.

- We pay for the sin of Adam and Eve. We are born innocent and remain that way until we reach the age of accountability.

- Our spiritual existence came into being at conception. God created the human race in need of salvation in which the majority would not reconcile. God knew this and did it anyway, therefore God is cruel and unloving.

- The serpent in Genesis was Satan. He took the form of an animal and was struck down on his belly to crawl as a snake.

- The enmity of Genesis 3:16 was between Christ and the devil.

- King Tyrus was Satan. Even though God told us King Tyrus was just a "mortal man" three times.

We ignore that because it does not fit "established doctrine."

- The Earth is six thousand years old. Under the obscuration, we must believe that because paleontologists tell us snakes have been crawling on their bellies for ninety million years. The true age of the Earth will throw off our doctrine under the obscuration.

- There was no death or disease before Adam and Eve. Therefore, the dinosaurs did not exist. The tyrannosaurus reassembled, and on display at the American Museum of Natural History has to be a deception from Satan to throw us off.

Above the obscuration (above the mystery) which is on God's side of the scroll.

- Adam and Eve brought sin into the world, which means they disobeyed God in the Garden. God knew this before they were created. The Bible tells us they brought sin into the world. It does not tell us they brought our sin into the world. We do not pay for their sin. We pay for our rebellion against God which happened before the foundation of the planet.

- Our spiritual creation happened long before the foundation of the planet. Ephesians 1:4 tells us this. Before the foundation of the planet, we lived in love and harmony with God.

- The serpent in Genesis was not the devil. That serpent was us. The serpent in Revelation 12:9 is a different serpent; it was the Archaios serpent. The "original" serpent. In Genesis, God was speaking to us the rebellion. We existed.

- The enmity of Genesis 3:16 is between man and woman. It is driven from the difference in our natures. God put the enmity between us as a protection.

- King Tyrus was not Satan or possessed by Satan. God told us this three times. "Tyrus, you are just a man." God told us King Tyrus was in the Garden. The only way that could happen is if he existed before his physical birth. That is from scripture. He did exist before his physical birth as did all of us. Under the obscuration this is not possible and therefore the story of Tyrus needs to be changed by the IC to bring it into compliance with established doctrine. Not one verse in the Bible supports King Tyrus was Satan, was possessed by Satan or had any connection to the entity of Satan. Tyrus was part of the embodiment of the serpent as were all of us.

- The Earth is not six thousand years old. It's not flat or the center of the universe either. The planet we live on is 4.5 billion years old.

- In the time before Adam and Eve, the Earth was a violent and deadly place. The dinosaurs were carnivores. They killed each other for food. They procreated, and they died of disease. There was death on this Earth before Adam. The dinosaurs were not compatible with the human race so God removed them. They served a purpose.

- The "death" Adam and Eve brought into the world was not physical death; it was spiritual death.

Again, we can reconcile with God and remain on our side of the scroll, but our knowledge of us and of God has been greatly skewed with man's truth. Our institutional leaders not only live in Isaiah 29:13, they are also the church of Laodicea. The lukewarm church God will spew out of His mouth. They have greatly damaged the truth. They have led the planet astray, even the elite.

Under the obscuration, many paradoxes are put in place which have no answer. We have seen many of these paradoxes listed in this book. Instead of repeating the paradoxes, let's look at something else. Many of us, church members, believers or anyone who reads the Bible have questions. When we do, we turn to our church leaders or online bible commentaries. On our side of the scroll, under the obscuration, much of scripture has no answer. One example (of many):

"Women will be saved through childbearing." — *1st Timothy 2:15 (NIV)*

Under the obscuration, this verse has little meaning. It's also an example of how corrupt our IC is. If we read online commentaries on this verse, we will read an endless amount of fluff and bluster. Many words with no meaning. After speaking to a church leader or reading one of the many commentaries you will be no closer to the truth. You can't be because the institutional church lives under the obscuration. Above the obscuration, this verse will make perfect sense. Many, many scriptures fall into this category. It's why so many church members don't trust church leadership. They cannot get even basic questions answered and are indeed discouraged from asking certain questions. Members are shamed by church leaders telling them they are questioning the sovereignty of God. They are not; they are questioning the wisdom of the leaders. They will not allow that. Church members are being deceived; they just don't know why. Understanding the two-sided scroll will answer this.

"And I saw a mighty angel proclaiming in a loud voice, "Who is worthy to break the seals and open the scroll?" 3 But no one in heaven or on earth or under the earth could open the scroll or even look inside it. 4 I wept and wept because no one was found who was worthy to open the scroll or look inside." — Revelation 5:2 (NIV)

This gives us an enormous amount of information. Again, the scroll alludes to God's plan. One in which we are not privy to or have full access to. The mystery He tells us will be lifted in the end days. The obscuration will be lifted. It's been hidden in plain sight all along in the scriptures. In all the verses, the IC has not put meaning to. There is far more.

The glory of God, God's nature, the love of God's character and the love God has for us is beyond our ability to fully grasp.

God's side of the scroll may be beyond our ability to grasp. The fact that there are two premises, two narratives, two sides, we can grasp that. It is in the Bible. It is for us to understand. For those who will listen.

"Now we see but a poor reflection as in a mirror; then we shall see face to face. Now I know in part; then I shall know fully, even as I am fully known." — 1 Corinthians 13:12 (NIV)

Revelation 14:3 tells us the 144,000 will sing a song no one can learn. Indeed, we can't because it's information beyond our capability. As is the full extent of this scroll. We can put meaning to the two sides but not the full plan.

I can't imagine the full extent of how God sees us. There is so much hate and evil on this planet. People treat each other in such a mean way. It's a hostile and toxic planet. It must pain God to witness His children treating each other the way they do. The worst offenders seem to be the ones who have wrapped themselves in religion.

This verse is one of many in which the IC bluffs about and adds many flowery words and lengthy commentaries, but at the end of which no meaning is put to it.

CHAPTER 8:

The Little Scroll

In Revelation 10, we are given a tremendous amount of information. Information which has been hidden from us since Apostle John wrote it two thousand years ago. If we understand what God has given us in this book, we can use it. We can prepare and understand the times we are in. If we continue with the endless amount of false information being given to us, we will never see. Not until it's too late.

Before we unravel this chapter, we need to go further back in the Bible and look at some other verses which will be answered in this chapter.

Jesus answered, "If I want him to remain alive until I return, what is that to you? You must follow me." 23 Because of this, the rumor spread among the believers that this disciple would not die. But Jesus did not say that he would not die; he only said, "If I want him to remain alive until I return, what is that to you?" —John 21:22 (NIV)

This is an interesting exchange between Jesus and Peter. This was after the resurrection so the "until I return" can be assumed the second coming. So, Apostle John will be alive when Jesus returns? That would mean he would have to be over two thousand years old. There is another explanation. The correct one.

"Truly I tell you; this generation will certainly not pass away until all these things have happened." — Matthew 24:34 (NIV)

"Truly I tell you; this generation will certainly not pass away until all these things have happened." — Luke 21:32 (NIV)

Things are not what they seem. Under our current paradigm, these verses make little sense. Meaning has been twisted into these two verses in Matthew and Luke. What Jesus said to Peter in the gospel of John has never been explained.

Keeping these verses in mind, let's look at Revelation 10 and read what it is really telling us.

"Then I saw another mighty angel coming down from heaven. He was robed in a cloud, with a rainbow above his head; his face was like the sun, and his legs were like fiery pillars. 2 He was holding a little scroll, which lay open in his hand. He planted his right foot on the sea and his left foot on the land." — Revelation 10:1 (NIV)

Remember, the end day prophecies were sealed until the end days. God told us this three times in the book of Daniel. Apparently, this does not suit mans' purpose or is yet again another commandment in which our institutional church leaders feel they can disobey with impunity. In an effort to appease its members, the IC will have an answer for this prophecy; it will be as false as the others. They tell us the little scroll was symbolic for ingesting knowledge that John will then in turn give out. They tell us the angels' feet being on the land and on the sea is symbolic of ownership or authority of the planet. Like most IC doctrine, it is completely false. What the institutional church tells us on these verses is complete nonsense. If we listen to them, we will gain absolutely no knowledge of God or of the prophecies. By attributing these prophecies to a symbolic gesture, we will never be able to put use to these scriptures. The truth will remain hidden. Man has made up an answer to a question they have not had the authority to answer. These prophecies were sealed. By their false doctrine, it has thrown off the true meaning to these passages. In a search of any biblical commentary, you will see the profound arrogance and self-righteousness of man. They are indeed leading the planet astray with their nonsense and shallow and superficial words.

Each word of these prophecies has meaning. They were written for us. Each word gives us information. Each has a purpose. They give us time reference and identification. If we read them and put true meaning to them, we will see where we are in time.

This angel didn't have his feet in different places; he had his feet in different times. Apostle John was taken from his time and put into our time. Apostle John will be here during the end days and will be certainly here when New York City is destroyed by a nuclear weapon.

When Jesus spoke to Peter in the gospel of John, he wasn't telling Peter that John would live until he returned; that would make him two thousand years old. He told him he would be alive when he returned. There is a difference. Jesus brought Apostle John forward into the future, possibly with others which may account for "this generation will certainly not pass away until these things have happened."

The angel did not have his feet in two different places. He had his feet in two different times. Apostle John will be here in the flesh.

Apostle John did not die and neither is he two thousand years old. We will see more proof of this as we read scripture. Ignore the false symbology from the institutional church leaders.

We are given information about this scroll the angel gives Apostle John. He tells us it's sweet to the taste but bitter to the stomach. This is a description of something we know about today. God was telling us something. God was giving us information we can use. Five times the scroll was mentioned. Five times! God is telling us something. The fact that we were told multiple times that the scroll would taste sweet and be sour to the stomach is also giving us information. Again, the repeated mention of this scroll and its effects on the human body was God trying to transfer information to us. He was telling us something!

Today, we have medicines doctors give to people who will be or have been exposed to nuclear radiation. The sweet taste and sour stomach match the side effects of some of the anti-radiation medicines. We were being told two things in these passages. We were being told Apostle John will be here in the flesh in these end days and that he will be exposed to nuclear radiation. In the next few chapters, we will prove in the scripture that the source of the radiation will come from the destruction of New York City. Apostle John will witness it.

3 "and he gave a loud shout like the roar of a lion. When he shouted, the voices of the seven thunders spoke. 4 And when the seven thunders spoke, I was about to write; but I heard a voice from heaven say, "Seal up what the seven thunders have said and do not write it down." (NIV)

This passage is again giving us useful information. We need to read it carefully to determine what we are being told. "Do not write it down." Think about this statement, "Do not write . . ." Apostle John could not have been in the spirit; if he were in a vision or a dream or some type of other state than in a physical state, he could not write anything down. Writing is a physical act, not a spiritual one. Apostle John was in the flesh when the angel spoke to him. When Apostle John wrote about the destruction of Mystery Babylon, (New York City), he was physically present. He was in person. He witnessed the nuclear bomb destroying New York City in real time. Something was hidden from us. This statement itself gives us information. This statement "do not write it down" has a meaning. It was written and recorded in the Bible to transfer information to us as the reader of God's Word. The vernacular itself was intentional and serves a purpose.

5 "Then the angel I had seen standing on the sea and on the land raised his right hand to heaven. 6 And he swore by him who lives for ever and ever, who created the heavens and all that is in them, the earth and all that is in it, and the sea and all that is in it, and said, "There will be no more delay! 7 But in the days when the seventh angel is about to sound his trumpet, the mystery of God will be accomplished, just as he announced to his servants the prophets." (NIV)

The mystery of God will reveal the tremendous amount of false teaching from our IC. We will see we have had it all wrong from the beginning, drastically wrong. We will see the wickedness of man and we will see the love and glory of our Creator. We will have the veil lifted from us and see clearly who we are and what our rebellion was. The institutional churches have set up an endless number of paradoxes which cannot be answered under the mystery. These paradoxes will be answered once the mystery is lifted.

". . . he will destroy the shroud that enfolds all peoples, the sheet that covers all nations;" — Isaiah 25.7 (NIV)

CHAPTER 9

Satan Thrown Out of Heaven

"A great sign appeared in heaven: a woman clothed with the sun, with the moon under her feet and a crown of twelve stars on her head. 2 She was pregnant and cried out in pain as she was about to give birth." — Revelation 12:1 (NIV)

In the established Christian doctrine as put forth by today's institutional church, this woman referenced in Revelation 12 is the nation of Israel. The child she gives birth to is Jesus. This is false. The book of Revelation was written long after the birth of Christ and long after his death. What is written here in Revelation is a prophecy. It is something which would not take place for two-thousand years. The IC has hidden the meaning to this prophecy because they could not make sense of it and therefore came up with something which would loosely fit with other scriptures. A plausible explanation, after all, who would question them?

The woman is a reference to a nation; yes, similar references have been made to the nation of Israel, but this cannot be Israel. The timing does not work. Some equate the sign in Heaven to astrological signs, alignment of bodies in the cosmos. The problem with this is that it will conflict with verse 3. If this sign is an astrological sign, then we would have to see another cosmic event matching verse 3.

The woman is not the nation of Israel or Mary, and the child is not Jesus. This prophecy is playing out in today's present time.

The woman is the United States; it will fit perfectly when we read the entire verse and put it into context with the other verses. Clothed in the sun is a spiritual reference. It was acknowledgement that our nation was founded on Christian principles and that our nation has believers in it. They are the iron in this deeply divided nation. Clothed in the sun could be no other nation because of the next part of the same verse, "the moon under her feet." Only one nation on this planet has had the moon under her feet. Our nation has a distinction; in that, it's the only nation on the planet in which its citizens have had men stand on the moon.

Again, the woman giving birth cannot be the birth of Christ; that's not an end day prophecy. The timing is off.

This nation is in great pain and has been for generations. The pain is born out in the secular progressive slip into an ungodly immoral nation. This nation has been killing babies for many years and has slid into this immoral degradation of sanctioning homosexual marriage. An immorality which is not only now legal but being forced upon us to be culturally acceptable. This nation has indeed been in the pain of childbearing for decades.

The twelve stars on her head is still a bit of a mystery. It could mean our nation was founded on Judean Christian values, but I am not sure enough to make a definitive statement about it. The definitive statement is that this woman is our nation. It is not Israel. Also, it is not a reference to any astrological signs.

"Then another sign appeared in heaven: an enormous red dragon with seven heads and ten horns and seven crowns on its' heads." — Revelation 12:3 (NIV)

This nation is losing this battle, this spiritual warfare. The "clay" in this country are the ungodly, the secular progressive movement away from God, and away from His commandments. The idealization of the homosexual life style and the acceptance of homosexual marriage. This nation in pain has killed seventy-two million babies. It is indeed in great pain. Through the dynamics of tribalism, the Leviathan spirit has gained a foothold. It has gained influence and control. The dragon giving "power" to the beast is the Leviathan spirit working within our human nature, within our tribalism. The dragon is us, not Satan the entity. Again, the dragon is the spirit of Satan, our rebellious nature. The dragon is us as is the serpent in Genesis 3. The IC is teaching Satan completely wrong.

This thing with the seven heads and ten horns is the fourth beast of Daniel which is also the beast of Revelation 13. It is the United States. The dragon is referenced in Revelation 13, "as the dragon stood on the shore." As in this verse, the dragon is a reference to the human spirit as influenced by Leviathan. That is the spirit in rebellion to God.

Because this is a modern-day reference, it cannot be Israel, nor can the baby be Jesus. More will be spoken of about this dragon in the chapter on Revelation 13.

Those who seek the truth will do well to disregard all the false information fed to them by the institutional church. They are hiding these prophecies.

"Its tail swept a third of the stars out of the sky and flung them to the earth. The dragon stood in front of the woman who was about

to give birth so that it might devour her child the moment he was born." — Revelation 12:4 (NIV)

In the established (accepted doctrine), the "tail sweeping a third of the stars" is understood as being the fall of Satan. The IC has accepted the "dragon" as being the entity of Satan. Not here, this dragon is us.

This verse does not say "stars swept out of heaven" but "out of the sky." This is of significance because it is not a spiritual reference but a political one. This prophecy has already happened. All of Revelation 12:4 has happened. Note the stars were flung to earth before the women gave birth.

The seven heads and ten horns are the United States. The dragon is not Satan but rather the congealment of our human nature as influenced by Leviathan. This spirit is visible in our current culture. It is our current culture. It is a reference to the "clay" in our deeply divided nation. It is the secular progressive ungodly movement which is against God and His commandments. The power of it is also visible in our conversations. Understanding this solves the mystery of why those on the left cannot be swayed in debate over their adherence to lies and propaganda. Debates that no doubt cause a great deal of frustration. That is the power of this Leviathan spirit.

To clarify this. The United States is the fourth beast of Daniel. It is a deeply divided nation made of iron and clay. The iron is those who follow Jesus and walk in faith with God. The "woman" is the iron. The clay is those who do not follow Jesus. They are the secular progressives, those opposed to God. They are the dragon. They are the ones, though the dynamics of tribalism are controlled by Leviathan, that spirit within us that oppose God and all those belonging to God. Leviathan is the spirit of Satan itself.

This "child" is not Christ. The woman is not Israel. The woman is this nation. The pain is the spiritual warfare raging in this country and on this planet. The child is Donald Trump.

The dragon, those controlled by Leviathan, tried to "devour" Trump before and after the presidential election. This prophecy has been fulfilled. The lies and the deceit, the spin and the propaganda. The weaponization of our intelligence agencies and of the law enforcement agencies was the attempt to devour this man. The dragon slinging the stars to the earth is a reference to the "deep state." Political forces in an attempt to prevent Trump from becoming President or to take him out if elected destroyed the lives of influential people. Those people were in Trump's orbit. They spared no expense destroying anyone supporting Trump.

When this country elected Donald Trump as President it was essentially a profound statement. Never in history has such a man been elected as President. This nation is in so much pain, indeed the planet is in pain. Almost desperately this country has been calling out. Trump's presidency has exposed a profound corruption in our political system. He has been greatly opposed before and after the election. Our corrupt political leaders have exposed themselves as has our main stream media, academia and the entertainment industry. They have gone through great lengths to destroy this man.

"She gave birth to a son, a male child, who "will rule all the nations with an iron scepter." And her child was snatched up to God and to his throne." —Revelation 12:5 (NIV)

Trump is under God's protection. We repeatedly see photos of Trump standing with Christian leaders who pray over him and pray with him. Trump's appointment was by God. Snatched up to the throne could not be a reference to the resurrection of Christ because that was past and this prophecy was future. The IC has this wrong. Rule the Earth with an iron scepter is a reference to the political, financial and military dominance President Trump had. It could only be this one leader to fulfill this prophecy.

"The woman fled into the wilderness to a place prepared for her by God, where she might be taken care of for 1,260 days." — Revelation 12:6 (NIV)

This is an incredible and significant verse for our future. For us. This woman is a nation, our nation. The woman is the United States. This verse has nothing to do with the nation of Israel being exiled. That was in the past and this is in the future. The timing does not work.

The clay is the dragon. The Iron are the followers of Jesus.

The 1,260 days is relevant, and it will be the amount of time we will need to live through the hell which is about to happen.

Just prior to the 1,260 days after President Trump was elected, a man in Minneapolis was killed by a police officer. Within a week, the entire nation erupted into national protests. The Leviathan spirit operating under the false guise of systemic racism stirred up those controlled by it. Through the dynamic of tribalism, the entire nation has turned lawless and violent. This prophecy has been fulfilled. The iron is now under attack from the Leviathan spirit as fueled by the next verse.

"Then war broke out in heaven. Michael and his angels fought against the dragon, and the dragon and his angels fought back. 8 But he was not strong enough, and they lost their place in heaven. 9 The great dragon was hurled down — that ancient serpent called the devil, or Satan, who leads the whole world astray. He was hurled to the earth, and his angels with him." — Revelation 12:7 (NIV)

This dragon is the Satan, the entity. The original word in this passage is Archaios serpent (not ancient). Archaios means, in this context, original. This entity has been on the sidelines from the beginning. Until now.

The IC views on this makes no logical sense for the timeline. This war which broke out is taking place in present day, not in the beginning as is taught. This dragon is not the serpent in Genesis 3.

This is a prophecy from Apostle John. It was not a past event; it was a future event relative to Apostle John's time. It is a significant understanding of what will happen. I believe it strongly it collates with the thirty minutes of silence in Heaven that we will see in another verse. When this happens, this planet will be a very different place than before Satan is thrown out. Indeed, it may already be underway. We see something play out in the news every night. Massive corruption being almost completely ignored by the mainstream media. Not only ignored but covered up. The spiritual connectivity of this Leviathan spirit is cohesive and directly linked with the secular progressive movement. The cultural shift which has dumbed down the fabric of our society is the clay in this deeply divided nation. The iron is those who follow Jesus. We are greatly outnumbered, and our religious leaders, many of them, have sold us out. They have sold the truth out. That is the spirit of antichrist. That was the spirit present in the third letter of John. Our leaders today, many of them, are Diotrephes. They are leading many astray as Jesus had told us they would.

Satan and his angels being "thrown down" is a present-day prophecy. Because God created this planet for us to live in our rebellion, He had to allow us to live outside of His embodiment. Up until this point of our existence Satan has been restricted. There is evidence in the Bible which supports this. Herod was an example. If

Satan had been unrestricted, Herod would not have had to kill all the young children. Had Satan had the influence many of our IC leaders tell us about, Satan would have known and killed Jesus. God would not and could not allow that. Herod did not have that level of spiritual knowledge directly from Satan nor do we have that level of direct spiritual connectivity to God. We cannot because we live in rebellion to God. Balaam was an example of this. He was identified as a true prophet, but his level of spiritual connectivity to God was shown in the fact that he went against God's will. When our leaders today make such a claim of spiritual connectivity, they fulfill the prophecy of speaking for God, "claiming to be messiah." We do not have that connectivity. They are lying to enhance their status. God calls us for His glory not ours. God uses us for His plan, not us for our plan, status or business model.

Our leaders today are all too willing to blame Satan for our fall and thus exonerate us. They remove our culpability. This is false. We are responsible for our own fall. We rebelled against God before the foundation of the planet. Our church leaders are leading many astray in their false doctrine.

When our leaders today claim God whispers in their ears and then sell us books which spew the obscuration, whose behalf are they really working on? When they use such statements to increase their own status and therefore "put one man above another," whose behalf are they really working on? Is it for the glory of God or the glory of men?

The misconception of our spiritual connectivity with God and its purpose as well as our understanding of Satan's true spiritual influence over us has been derived by a complete lack of understanding as to who we really are. The entire premise is wrong. Our natures are a reflection of our rebellion. It is not Satan who influences us; it is our nature. It is why Apostle John referred to himself in Revelation 13 as the dragon. He was speaking to his fallen nature. As was Jesus when He said "get behind me Satan" when he spoke to Peter. He was speaking to Peter's fallen nature not the red man with the pitch fork. Our entire premise of Satan is off. Our entire premise of who we are is off. Our entire premise of why we are here is off.

"Then I heard a loud voice in heaven say: "Now have come the salvation and the power and the kingdom of our God, and the authority of his Messiah. For the accuser of our brothers and sisters, who accuses them before our God day and night, has been hurled down." — Revelation 12:10 (NIV)

Satan, the original serpent, and his angels get removed from Heaven and are cast down to this planet with us. This means, the "experiment" is now over. All the time leading up until now has been set for this stage.

To understand this accusation, one need only to read and understand the book of Job.

There has been a spiritual warfare which has been raging on this planet from the beginning. We have been in the tribulation since Adam was ejected from the Garden of Eden. Those who belong to God and who reject the spirit of the rebellion have been persecuted from the beginning. "Blessed are those who are hated because of me," Jesus told us about this dichotomy of people, that is those belonging to God and those belonging to Satan. In the gospel, John 8:44 he tells us about this dichotomy as well.

Those who belong to God are under, and have been under, spiritual attack from the beginning. The gospel of John 16:33 tells us, "In this world you will have tribulation." It's in our human nature to resist God and all that is of God. Our human nature is a terrible thing.

God knew this about us. "Love one another" was driven from the knowledge God had of our natures. Jesus knew how incredibly mean the humans are to each other, always looking for faults and weaknesses. Reduce someone else's status and increase our own. It's the rules of tribalism. It is in our nature to accuse each other day and night. If you belong to God and express it, by default you will not belong to the tribe of the rebellion and therefore will be attacked. The nature lives in all of us. Peter was a good example of this; he still had his fallen nature within him. Jesus pointed that out. So did Judas.

Those who reconcile with God still are subjugated to their fallen nature. The "new" nature does not make us perfect; if that were the case, we could not sin after reconciling with God. God told us that would not be the case. The book of Romans tells us this.

We reconcile with God for the original "sin" of rebellion against Him. According to scripture, we will always be subjugated to our human nature. "All things are legal for me" means our behavioral sins will not be held against those who reconcile with God for that original sin. We have it all wrong.

"They triumphed over him by the blood of the Lamb and by the word of their testimony; they did not love their lives so much as to shrink from death. 12 Therefore rejoice, you heavens and you who dwell in them! But woe to the earth and the sea, because the devil has gone down to you! He is filled with fury, because he knows that his time is short." —Revelation 12:11 (NIV)

Satan, the original serpent, the leader of the rebellion against God is now with us on this planet. Him and his angels.

Very contrary to established doctrine, this had not happened when Apostle John had written these prophecies. Remember, it was a prophecy. If you look at it as such, this entire chapter comes into focus.

Again, this is a present-day prophecy. It is bad news for the Earth's inhabitants. It means our rebellion is coming to an end.

In today's church services, a great deal of emphasis is put on the crucifixion. The death of Jesus seems to be reduced to euphemisms. Shallow and superficial doctrines. Perhaps under the obscuration this was necessary, providing the amount of information allowing those who belong to Jesus to reconcile with God. It is not just the death of Christ we should focus on but His life. The very existence of Jesus on this planet will not fully be understood under the obscuration. How could it be? The murder of Christ and salvation through him was prophesied. His life and the reason for it needs to be understood from the perspective above the obscuration. If not for the life of Jesus, His very existence on this planet, there would not have been that connection to God after our rebellion. We rebelled against God, we were put here on this planet because of it, to live apart from Him because that is what we wanted. Jesus being sent here was and is God telling us we can still reconcile that rebellion. It is what our salvation is. Not the euphemistic and shallow doctrine our IC leaders tell us. We reconcile with God through Christ. His life is what we need to focus on. The purpose of Christ being here has meant God has not forsaken us. We certainly do not deserve it. That is the loving God, not the one the IC is telling us about. We deserve nothing. God did not create a planet in which the majority would not reconcile with Him. That would be a cruel and unloving God. Salvation though Christ, the existence of Jesus on this planet is the blessed hope, the only hope those who rebelled have, which is all of us. The existence of Christ is the very real example of the love God has for us even though we rejected Him. That's the true

God, not the one the IC has told us of. That god created a planet in which the vast majority of people would be sentenced to Hell.

"When the dragon saw that he had been hurled to the earth, he pursued the woman who had given birth to the male child." — Revelation 12:13 (NIV).

The woman is those in this nation who belong to God, the iron, the believers. Satan does hate those who belong to God. The spirit of Satan which is the nature of those who live unreconciled with God hate us as well.

This original Satan, the leader of the rebellion is our enemy. The "woman" he pursues is us, those belonging to God. Trump was appointed by God. They tried to stop him before he became President and tried to remove him after the election. They failed. Now they will go after us. We will all be persecuted.

"The woman was given the two wings of a great eagle, so that she might fly to the place prepared for her in the wilderness, where she would be taken care of for a time, times and half a time, out of the serpent's reach." — Revelation 12:14 (NIV)

This is a very significant prophecy. An entire chapter will be devoted to it. Time, Times and a half a time, chapter 15.

"Then from his mouth the serpent spewed water like a river, to overtake the woman and sweep her away with the torrent. 16 But the earth helped the woman by opening its mouth and swallowing the river that the dragon had spewed out of his mouth. 17 Then the dragon was enraged at the woman and went off to wage war against the rest of her offspring — those who keep God's commands and hold fast their testimony about Jesus." — Revelation 12:15 (NIV)

This is an incredible prophecy. In the end times, the spiritual connectivity of the serpent will increase many fold, certainly after the "original serpent" the devil and his angels are thrown down. Things are about to get really bad on this planet; it's already starting. Watching the current events happening on this planet seem to defy all logic and rational. It is the Leviathan spirit we see. It's the river from the dragon we see in the news every night. The dragon has the Leviathan spirit in it, the connectivity of those in rebellion of Christ, the nature of man living in his rebellion. It will be made much worse after Satan is cast down. We are seeing this now. "Those who keep God's commandments" are those who have reconciled. The parishioners in the churches, not necessarily many of the leaders.

CHAPTER 10:

The Virus from the Abyss

1 The fifth angel sounded his trumpet, and I saw a star that had fallen from the sky to the earth. The star was given the key to the shaft of the Abyss. (NIV)

In the time before the foundation of the planet, we lived with God, all in harmony and love. Ephesians 1:4 tell us this. God tells us this. Gods created beings had no knowledge of what life would be like without Him. The entity of Satan, the Archaios serpent, the original rebel, thought of an existence better than that one in which we lived in the embodiment of our Creator. In this existence, we could live as our own gods. We could live free from God's authority and pursue an independent existence. Satan was wrong; we were wrong. We fell. We rebelled against our Creator and rejected Him. God knew what existence would be like without Him. Now we know, we live in it. God knew how vile and evil His created being could be not under His control, living as our own gods. We are all free to pursue this existence. This self-centered existence is one in which we live in, one in which we are free to pursue the thing which motivated us to fall. It is one in which we put ourselves at the center. The God has let us be. He has had very little interference in our pursuit. He had to so we would know. The entity of Satan, the Archaios serpent, the leader of the rebellion also has had little to no influence on the human race. This is contrary to what the established Christian doctrine tells us. Never the less, it is true. We were told this. Satan will not even be on the planet until the very end.

Most of the references in God's word to Satan are not references to the Archaios serpent; they are to us. When Jesus said to Peter, "get behind me Satan," he was making a reference to Peter's nature. When Jesus told the leader he "belonged to his father Satan," it was a reference to his nature. When Satan said to God, "I go to and fro on the planet and walk up and down on the face of it," it was a reference to the humans on the planet who lived in their rebellion to God.

Contrary to "established" Christian doctrine, the entity of The Satan does not influence us. The references to Satan in the Bible are to our own natures, not the original rebel who has been on the sideline from the beginning, as has God.

The star that was thrown from Heaven is explained to us in Revelation 12. Satan will not arrive in the flesh until the end. That is in the bible.

Contrary to established doctrine, the "Abyss" is not a direct reference to Hell, of which Satan has no authority. The Abyss is a reference to those on this planet living in rebellion. We are the Abyss. It is driven from the Satan nature of which we have all been apart since the rebellion before the foundation of the planet.

The "sea," the restless sea, the sea of people on this planet, can be controlled. Populations, societies, cultures, can all be controlled. This ability to control has always been with us, it is more prevalent and visible today than any time in our history. Certainly, this control has been seen in the past. It is how Hitler was able to congeal an entire society with lies and propaganda. Fear and tribalistic rules were the tools. This has always been with us. It is how the Leviathan controls the hearts and minds of its members. Satan being given the "key to the shaft" is telling us Satan will influence this tribalism of the Leviathan. Satan does not have authority, nor has God given him authority in this chapter. The "keys to the shaft of the Abyss" is Satan using his knowledge of us and our natures to control us. Some will recognize this and resist. Many will not and adhere to the new tribal rules. Those rules we are seeing playing out every day of our lives. Revelation 12 tells us, "But woe to the earth and the sea" because Satan will be thrown down. This is what the Abyss is, not the geographically place taught as Hell.

2 When he opened the Abyss, smoke rose from it like the smoke from a gigantic furnace. The sun and sky were darkened by the smoke from the Abyss. (NIV)

Even before Satan arrived on this planet, it has been a wicked place inhabited by man in rebellion to God. If the spirit of man were allowed to congeal, man would display a wickedness seen only in the time of Noah. Indeed, it had congealed in that time. God destroyed the planet because of it.

The Leviathan was destroyed, the Bible tells us this. In that time the offspring of the Nephilim dominated the planet and congealed the spirit in rebellion to God. God told us He "regretted making man." God was telling us something. It is explained in the book of Jude. Those "sons of God" who married the human females were the angels who lost their authority. The effect of the congealment through their offspring even took God by surprise. That is why He mentioned the "regret." It did not go as planned, and He had to destroy the planet. This congealment was not part of God's plan. It was not supposed to happen that quickly. We only "regret" when we make a mistake or something does not go as planned. God did not make a mistake, the Nephilim did.

Today it has congealed once again, as in the time of Noah. This time it will be far worse due to the direct influence the Archaios Satan will have on the planet. Woe to the Earth indeed! We are about to see the action of this Abyss as it plays out in front of us.

3 And out of the smoke locusts came down on the earth and were given power like that of scorpions of the earth. (NIV)

The smoke from the Abyss is the evil which has come from the congealment of the human spirit. We live in it. The COVID-19 virus was made by man. The evil of man manufactured this virus through "gain of function" which allowed an animal virus to be transmittable to humans. The locust is the COVID-19 virus. It was made by man; the Abyss is the spirit of the rebellion against God. Thus, the locusts came from the Abyss.

The mention of the "scorpion" is extremely important. It will be mentioned three times. The "sting" from the scorpion is the COVID-19 vaccine, which is not a vaccine. It is a gene therapy medicine which has never been attempted. It is poison.

4 They were told not to harm the grass of the earth or any plant or tree, but only those people who did not have the seal of God on their foreheads. (NIV)

This verse gives us a huge amount of information. The 144 thousand had the seal, no one else. Neither the virus nor the vaccine will affect them, they are protected. The rest of the planet will be subjugated to it. Many believers will receive the vaccine. They should not but will not lose their salvation because of it. It is not a litmus test for believers. We are told it will not harm the grass, plants or trees. What this is telling us is that it is not a "locust" in the way we look at locust. This "locust" is a virus which will only be transmittable to animals and humans. The mention of the locust not harming the vegetation is important. It tells us it is a virus which only affect mammals. It is the COVID-19 virus. The virus is not a grasshopper.

This locust came from the Abyss and is now here. It came from the evil heart of man. The COVID-19 virus came from an evil. It was manufactured by man. China developed it with the financial backing of the United States.

5 They were not allowed to kill them but only to torture them for five months. And the agony they suffered was like that of the sting of a scorpion when it strikes. (NIV)

The "sting" of the scorpion is a reference to the vaccine shot. Both the virus and the vaccine are referenced in this chapter. The five months is mentioned twice. It is significant. I believe this is telling us they are not allowed to "kill them" immediately. Something happens for five months. Either they recover after five months or most likely die after five months of suffering. This suffering will also lead into the plague which kills many on this planet. Since the "sting" of the scorpion is mentioned, it may be a combination of the vaccine and the virus. I believe, since the virus kills such a low percent of those who get it, it will be the vaccine which will kill many. It is possible the virus will mutate to a much more deadly strain; it is not likely a mutation which would kill a third of mankind which would be needed to fulfil the prophecy in verse 15. My understanding of this verse is that the vaccine will interact at some point in the bodies of all males who take the vaccine. We will see this is when we understand Isaiah 4:1 to be a demographic gender shift. We will get back to this.

6 "During those days people will seek death but will not find it; they will long to die, but death will elude them." (NIV)

This will be human suffering we have never seen; one way or another, it is man-made. The "vaccine" which is not a vaccine is extremely dangerous. Much more so than the COVID-19 virus itself.

7 "The locusts looked like horses prepared for battle. On their heads they wore something like crowns of gold, and their faces resembled human faces." (NIV)

8 "Their hair was like women's hair, and their teeth were like lions' teeth." (NIV)

We have all seen the common depiction of the COVID-19 virus. If we look at a graphic of the virus and read this passage, we can see a stark depiction. It looks like a head with hair, as this verse states. It is commonly depicted with red, blue and gold (or yellow). This is too much of a coincidence. Whatever kills a third of the planet has to be global, as the virus and the vaccine is. On top of the global presence, we are given an exact description of the virus itself. There is more, we will be given a description of the vaccine as well. The scorpion stings.

9 "They had breastplates like breastplates of iron, and the sound of their wings was like the thundering of many horses and chariots rushing into battle." (NIV)

There are two components to this virus. First, it was man-made. China manipulated an animal virus through gain of function technology. This allowed humans to be infected by it and transmit it to other humans. What they did was evil. The second component to this is the vaccine. The vaccine is man-made. Not only that it is not really even a vaccine, it's an experimental RNA medicine. "Thundering of many horses" is loud. This is telling us something.

There is a very loud cry going out now day and night. The cry is to compel the vaccine. To the point our government is violating our constitution and our civil liberties to make us take this experimental medicine. Employers are firing employees for not taking the shot. This is the many horses. If this is the case, which I believe what this passage is telling us, then the vaccine component to this equation is relevant. As is the five months.

There is another fascinating reference in this verse, fascinating. There is a mention of "iron."

This is important as the COVID-19 virus has a component to it, iron!

Although there may be a dispute as to the effect of this "iron overload," there is no dispute iron is a component of the virus.

10 "They had tails with stingers, like scorpions, and in their tails they had power to torment people for five months." (NIV)

This is important. Again, the five months. We know the vaccines have had an effect on some people, both men and women. Different effects. Woman seem to be prone to blood clots. Men seem to be prone to heart inflammation, mostly young men. They don't know why. Most recover. The fact this is happening is telling us it is having an interaction in our bodies they don't understand, nor do they know the long-term effect.

The scorpion sting is the vaccine shot.

The vaccine will soon cause a reaction in our bodies. It looks to be only men, not the initial reaction, but the delayed reaction. The fact that the males have had the heart the inflammation, it will be an indication of what will come. Heart inflammation is a symptom of chromosome disease. The vaccine will kill males, as will be supported in scripture.

We are told it will be bad for the pregnant women and nursing mothers. We are told of the demographic gender shift in Isaiah 4:1. We will look at the math on this shortly.

11 "They had as king over them the angel of the Abyss, whose name in Hebrew is Abaddon and in Greek is Apollyon (that is, Destroyer)." (NIV)

The king over them, (the locust)? This can't be a reference to Satan. Why would the Bible title Satan in this way? No other time in the Bible is Satan listed this way. It is not Satan. Therefore, it is someone else. It reads king over them, not king of the Abyss. King of the locust. I believe we can identify this Apollyon. There is one man who has been a part of this locust and the scorpion sting from the beginning. Someone who provided funding to the Chinese for the gain of function research and apparently lied to Congress about it. Someone out in front pushing the vaccine, someone supporting the mandates. I believe this Apollyon is Anthony Fauci. It would mean he will have the deaths of over two billion people on his hands.

12 "The first woe is past; two other woes are yet to come." (NIV)

13 "The sixth angel sounded his trumpet, and I heard a voice coming from the four horns of the golden altar that is before God." (NIV)

14 "It said to the sixth angel who had the trumpet, "Release the four angels who are bound at the great river Euphrates." (NIV)

15 "And the four angels who had been kept ready for this very hour and day and month and year were released to kill a third of mankind." (NIV)

This can only be caused by the common thread of the COVID-19 vaccine. In the next chapter, we will look at this more in depth. In order for a third of the planet to die, something would have to be common globally. No disease has ever been lethal enough to kill a third of the population globally. The COVID-19 virus would not come close to this. It is the vaccine. It is global.

16 "The number of the mounted troops was twice ten thousand times ten thousand. I heard their number." (NIV)

Only one army on the planet will come close to this number. A two-hundred-million-man army. China is the only country on the planet with an army this size. It is no coincident that this is mentioned in this chapter. China has a significant role in the evil which is playing out on this planet. They manipulated an animal virus and made it transmissible to humans. Presumably to make a bio-weapon. Why would they do such an evil thing? Why would our country fund it? China has infiltrated our government, our corporations and our media. China is an evil country which is doing an inordinate amount of damage to our country and to the world. Our corrupt politicians have allowed this to happen. Our corrupt media is covering for this evil.

The "key to the shaft of the Abyss" is how Satan is influencing the planet. The key to the shaft is a reference to the means of which the evil is controlling. The corrupt media, the corrupt politicians, the corrupt law enforcement agencies like the FBI and the CIA, corrupt corporations and the corrupt social media platforms. They are all controlling the information flow and culture through means of tribalistic behavior. This is how Leviathan has received its power. The human spirit has been congealed against God, as in the times of Noah.

Our institutional church organizations are a part of this. Todays organized church is the church of Laodicean. There doctrines are false and are hiding the truth. Their doctrines are based on man's truth, and God's Word is twisted into sound business practices which allow them to thrive. They are the ones claiming to be Messiah and leading the many astray. God told us He would "spew them out of His mouth."

Today's established Christian doctrine is contrary to God, as the prophet Isaiah told us it would be, as Jesus told us it would be. It is why no one is listening. Not yet.

17 "The horses and riders I saw in my vision looked like this: Their breastplates were fiery red, dark blue, and yellow as sulfur. The heads of the horses resembled the heads of lions, and out of their mouths came fire, smoke and sulfur." (NIV)

Verse 8 gave us a description of the COVID-19 virus. Verse 17 does as well, much more detailed. Although the color of the virus may not be known accurately, the common that are depicted of this virus will match exactly this verse. This is too much of a coincidence. Blue red and yellow.

Fire, smoke and sulfur. Better known as Pfizer, Moderna and Johnson & Johnson.

18 "A third of mankind was killed by the three plagues of fire, smoke and sulfur that came out of their mouths." (NIV)

The three plagues coming out of their mouths. This cannot be a coincidence. This has to be a reference to the three vaccines. Out of their mouths come death. The vaccines are the scorpion sting. A third of mankind is about to die. It is not the virus that will kill this third; it is the vaccine.

20 "The rest of mankind who were not killed by these plagues still did not repent of the work of their hands; they did not stop worshiping demons, and idols of gold, silver, bronze, stone and wood — idols that cannot see or hear or walk." (NIV)

This is an incredible passage. Even after all this people will remain blind. They will follow their motivation of the fall and live in rebellion against God. So strong is Leviathan, so strong is the hatred of God. People will still hold on to being their own god's.

21 "Nor did they repent of their murders, their magic arts, their sexual immorality or their thefts." (NIV)

We rebelled with no knowledge of what life would be like without God, a life in which we could be our own god. We have no memory of life with God which was God's plan from the beginning. This is the tribulation, life unbiased from our memories of Ephesians 1:4. Unbiased from God. Unbiased from the Archaios Serpent. This planet and what has happened to it has been driven strictly by man and our Satan nature. This is what God had to show us.

The murders are the massive number of abortions. The magic arts are not "black magic"; they are a reference to today's incessant use of our devices, mostly the obsession of the young which allows them to live in an alternate reality. For the sexual immorality, one needs to go no further than a brief online search. Maybe more than any time in history has sexual perversion been more prevalent today. All manner of evil is now available. The thefts are the reference to the complete out-of-control corruption thriving on this planet.

We have been in the tribulation for six thousand years. It is coming to an end.

CHAPTER 11

Calculating the Death from the Abyss

We need to look at three Bible passages to fully understand the ominous COVID-19 virus. A virus for which a vaccine will kill a third of mankind. We can even get a basic time frame of these deaths.

The first is from Isaiah:

In that day seven women will take hold of one man and say, "We will eat our own food and provide our own clothes; only let us be called by your name. Take away our disgrace!" — Isaiah 4:1 (NIV)

No meaning has ever been put to this verse by our established doctrine. We are told by the IC that this verse is a typo, that it was miscategorized; it belongs in chapter three with the petulant women not chapter four. This makes no sense and is false. A female saying, she will buy her own food and make her own clothes is not the sign of a petulant female. The geographic location of Isaiah chapter 4 is Israel. This verse is telling us of a demographic swing. In Israel, the gender demographic will change from its current state of 50.5%

male/49.5% female to 12.5% male/87.5% female. That is a big shift. This verse is telling us something very ominous. Millions of men in Israel will die. The deaths will not come from military actions; the demographic would not change that much. Something else will kill these men. Something which will be common to the entire planet, the plague of fire, smoke and sulfur. The three plagues of the COVID-19 vaccine. The vaccines will interact inside the male body and kill them. We will get to these numbers. Keep in mind, this verse is giving us a clue of what will happen. One of many.

The next passage is from 2 Thessalonians:

"The coming of the lawless one will be in accordance with how Satan works. He will use all sorts of displays of power through signs and wonders that serve the lie, 10 and all the ways that wickedness deceives those who are perishing. They perish because they refused to love the truth and so be saved. 11 For this reason God sends them a powerful delusion so that they will believe the lie. 12 and so that all will be condemned who have not believed the truth but have delighted in wickedness." — 2 Thessalonians 2:9 (NIV)

The "lie" is the COVID-19 vaccine. It is poison. Today, they are lying about the effectiveness of the vaccines which seem to not work after six months. They dismiss and criticize the use of therapeutics, even restrict the use of life saving medicine. They over inflate the death rate of COVID-19 while denying the therapeutics. They dismiss the natural immunity of those who have recovered from the virus. They are forcing people against their will to take these vaccines. The mandates are causing people to lose their jobs or take a medicine they do not want.

The third passage comes from Revelation;

"A third of mankind was killed by the three plagues of fire, smoke and sulfur that came out of their mouths." — Revelation 9: 18 (NIV)

The scorpion sting is the vaccine shot. The three plagues of the fire, smoke and sulfur are the three vaccines which are now being used.

With these three passages and looking at the current vaccine numbers, both worldwide and for Israel, we can see where we are in time. We need to look at Israel because the gender demographic change in Isaiah 4:1 is for Israel, and the death of the third of mankind is worldwide.

If we see the gender demographic change in Israel represents the deaths of males and make the assumption that the third of mankind dying will follow suit, we can understand the prophecy.

What could kill so many people? Something has to have a global commonality. We see a detailed description of the COVID-19 virus in Revelation 9. The virus itself is common globally. But the virus itself cannot fulfill the prophecy of killing a third of the planet. It is not that lethal. It kills far less than one percent of those infected. Which would be far less lethal if our corrupt politicians were not playing politics with the COVID-19 treatments.

So, what else is common globally? The vaccine is. It is not really a vaccine; it is an experimental mRNA medicine which has never been tried on humans. All prior mRNA attempts have failed. Now they are trying this experiment on a global scale. It will fail.

Because of the demographic shift in Israel will be caused by the death of the men, there has to be a commonality in men but not in females. There is very little genetic difference between the male and female bodies. The chromosomes being the most obvious difference. The male has XY, while the female has XX. It would follow that the negative effect in the male's body would stem from what the female does not have, the Y chromosome. Possible something else, but that seems to be the most obvious.

The vaccines will cause a chromosome disease in men. Most if not all males injected with this vaccine will die. We can prove this in the scripture and with the COVID-19 vaccine numbers provided by the CDC.

If we look at the vaccination numbers, we can see how close we may be to this mass extinction event.

First, we look at Israel. Today is October 18, 2021. They have vaccinated 63% of their population.

The total population is 7,733,144. The male population over fourteen is 2,811,770. The current gender demographic is 50.5% male and 49.5% female as previously stated. To shift to 12.5 male and 87.5 female, the male population between fifteen and sixty-five years old (roughly the age women would approach a man) would have to drop to 348,911. If we make an assumption that all men who have the plague injected will die, and assuming roughly the same number of males and females take the shot, the vaccine injecting rate would have to be 81%. The current rate is 63% (but 78% of those over the age of 14). In about six months, they will hit the 81%. If we look at the global numbers, and assume the six months, the global vaccine will match almost exactly.

Global population is 7,962,119,434. Above the age of fourteen, the population is 6,016,180,324. (We look at the age above fourteen to get a more accurate vaccine percent).

The global vaccine percent of fully vaccinated people is 49%. If we assume the same percent of males and females have taking the shot, and if we assume that all males will die who have received the shot, the world vaccination rate would have to reach 66% to attain the third of mankind dying. Again, it works out to just over six months from today's date. Same as Israel.

The Bible tells us the "affliction" will last five months. After which the third of mankind will die. This is what is about to happen; in the spring of next year, estimating April or May (maybe sooner), those first vaccinated (males) will start exhibiting symptoms of an illness never seen before. My guess is that a gene or a series of genes on the males Y chromosome will mutate or somehow become compromised. They will suffer greatly. Five months later, they will die. The death rate will start increasing late next fall. Something else will happen. Once the illness is identified as being caused by the COVID-19 vaccine, the vaccine injections will be immediately stopped, which will freeze the death rate at the one-third of mankind and will also freeze the death rate in Israel to attain the 7:1 ratio.

This planet will change drastically. The prophecy will be fulfilled, and the wickedness of man will be exposed.

The gender demographic of Israel is clear. The one-third of mankind dying will match the vaccine percent relative to Israel to match their vaccine rate which is much higher than the global rate. The vaccine is the only global commonality.

The majority if not all males who take this vaccine will die.

With this knowledge, we can put understanding to the following passages;

19 "How dreadful it will be in those days for pregnant women and nursing mothers!" (NIV)

These women will be without husbands. The vaccine will kill them. They will have very little support. The society, the family, the economy, our governments and the world in the aggregate will have collapsed.

20 "Pray that your flight will not take place in winter or on the Sabbath." (NIV)

The winter is not a reference to the season of the year; it is a reference to the elderly. With the large number of males on the planet dead, they will, like the pregnant females, have little to no support.

CHAPTER 12

Beast with the Ten Horns and Seven Heads

"The dragon stood on the shore of the sea. And I saw a beast coming out of the sea. It had ten horns and seven heads, with ten crowns on its horns, and on each head a blasphemous name." — Revelation 13:1 (NIV)

There is something remarkable about how this verse has been translated. Three different ways. The NIV reads the dragon stood on the shore. The others say "I stood," and others say "he stood." In some of the commentaries, this is mentioned. It explains this anomaly as Satan in the third person. It doesn't seem it could be both Satan and Apostle John. It is not well explained. There is another way of seeing this, it is both Satan, in a way, and Apostle John. If Apostle John references himself as the dragon, he is not admitting to being Satan, but Apostle John is telling us something. Satan is not who we think he is. The dragon is not who we think he is. The antichrist that Apostle John wrote about in his letters is not who we think either. The IC is that far off about Satan. Profoundly far off. This dragon is directly related to what Jesus said to Peter. Get behind me Satan. That was not a reference to the "devil." In Corinthians, Paul mentions about not getting married, and if you do, submit to each other so Satan does not tempt you. We might look at this as an actual statement of the devil himself tempting us. He in person tempts men into adulterous affairs because the wife does not submit. This is the institutional churches view on Satan. It is monstrously incorrect. These references to Satan or the dragon or the serpent in the book of Genesis are references to our own nature. The embodiment of the rebellion we came from. It does not mean the "devil" does not exist and as an individual entity. Revelation 12 tells us that entity will be thrown down in the end days. There seems to be an organization or a hierarchy in which the Satan is part of. These other references identify who we are and where we came from. We are not innocent, nor were we born innocent. The dragon is a reference to us.

When God spoke to the serpent in Genesis 3 and said, "Cursed are you above all cattle . . . on your belly you will crawl," He was not speaking to this singular entity, the "devil"; He was speaking to us. As is Apostle John speaking to the spirit of Satan, which is us. This is also the way Satan has been taught in the Jewish faith. We seem to have forgotten that. The Jews taught this correctly.

Everything I have done the last ten years points in the same direction. It is "man" and organized institutional religion that is way off. The doctrine of the institutions is massively off. God has allowed this as He allowed the Scribes and Pharisees to teach false doctrine for so many generations. God allowed the Catholic Church to do the same four hundred years ago; for generations they taught their false doctrine. We really need to understand this. If man has that direct communication with God, "commonality of the spirit through established doctrine" which all of our church leaders claim today, then how could these earlier churches have been so far off? And how are we any different today? We are not; we are following in the footsteps of all leaders before us. According to the IC, the reason we are here is to have us "harvest souls" to God while leaving countless billions to perish. This is false doctrine. If this were true, God would intervene when the institutional doctrine goes astray. He has not. Many, many generations prove this to be the case. Our entire history on this planet proves this to be the case. We put ourselves here on this planet when we rebelled against God before the foundation of the world. If this were not true, God would intervene, and He would show Himself directly to us. He would have angels convince us of His existence. He does not and man's doctrine is off.

It is why this verse has never been understood. The dragon is us, or at least, we are a part of it. That is what Apostle John is telling us.

The planet has drifted beyond the point of no return. Satan and his angels have been cast down. It is why little is making sense today. In the traditional view of Satan, Revelation 12 will make little sense. The IC ignores it; they have no answer. All the IC leaders are teaching doctrine which is profoundly off. They are not listening.

The beast with the seven heads and ten horns is the United States. Something which we covered in great depth in *Cursed Above All Cattle*. It fits perfectly with the book of Daniel. We are the fourth beast of Daniel.

"The beast I saw resembled a leopard, but had feet like those of a bear and a mouth like that of a lion. The dragon gave the beast his power and his throne and great authority." — Revelation 13:2 (NIV)

The leopard, bear and lion are descriptions of the military, political and financial might the United States holds.

The dragon is not "the devil" it is us. It is a reference to the nature of our rebellion in which Leviathan will live and give power to our culture through the power of tribalism. The dragon will give power to the beast. The dragon is our rebellious nature that will give power to the beast in the form of tribalism. It is why so much doesn't make sense today. It is how the secular progressive ideological propaganda works. The culture which will attack God and all those who belong to Him. The culture that attacks the values and faith of God's people. This power flows from the Leviathan in our natures. We are not innocent. The IC's understanding of Satan is about as far off as its understanding of the antichrist.

"There is no one who understands, there is no one who seeks God." —Romans 3:11 (NIV)

The dragon is us, the collective of our natures. Like fluid flow, we are linked instantly now by all of our devices. This is how our spirits have congealed through Leviathan. Against God. Controlled by the ancient serpent once he is thrown down. This planet is about to go through a pain never seen in human history. A pain brought about by our own doing. As Revelation 9 told us, Satan will have the "Keys to the Abyss." This means, Satan will control this congealment against God by controlling the narrative through the use of tribalism. This tribalism which is in opposition to God is the Leviathan. It was destroyed in the time of Noah as it will be destroyed in the end days.

Putting truth to this beast will seem unpatriotic and therefore will be hidden by the institutional church as it will have an adverse effect on their business models. Jesus told us they would lead many astray.

"One of the heads of the beast seemed to have had a fatal wound, but the fatal wound had been healed. The whole world was filled with wonder and followed the beast." — Revelation 13:3 (NIV)

Apostle John wrote this after the wound was healed. We can pin point this in a few scriptures. The wound is an economic one. New York City will be destroyed by a nuclear device, but its destruction is not this wound. That happens most likely after the recovery. There will be a rational for this. In order for us to heal the wound, our industry needs to return to this country which means the brunt of the economic pain will be felt by the countries that own our current debt and current manufacturing. They will have incentive to drop a nuke on us, not out of revenge but out of economic survival.

The timeline on this chapter seems to have an intentional overlap. "One of the heads" of the beast is a reference to a specific political administration. The beast is the United States, and the head refers to the leader. From other scriptures we see, there will be an economic collapse, the black horse with the scales. It may be an assumption to identify this wounded head with that prophecy, but it will fit with that verse and others. We will see this in verse 5.

This head being wounded could be something other than the economic collapse. It could be a political wound which we can argue has already happened with the impeachment of Trump. The problem with this is that there seems to be no other supporting scripture for it as there is for the economic collapse.

The wounding could also mean the destruction of New York City. That will happen. New York City will be destroyed by a nuclear weapon. We will see this when we decipher Revelation 17 and 18. The problem with this is that the timing doesn't seem to fit or at least the sequence of it. The wound seems to happen before New York City is destroyed.

"People worshiped the dragon because he had given authority to the beast, and they also worshiped the beast and asked, "Who is like the beast? Who can wage war against it?"—Revelation 13:4 (NIV)

No country can wage war against the United States. The dragon is the collection of the awful natures driven by Leviathan. Today's woke culture is an example of this Leviathan, the spirit opposed to God.

The worship of this beast is not a "religious" worship. It is a recognition of economic superiority. It exists now and has been in existence for many years now, as the United States has been at the center of most world economic and business activity. We need to see this verse in time context of the previous verse. After the head of the beast is wounded, it will recover and become an even more important economic powerhouse. This again leads to evidence of the wounding as an economic wounding. The United States over the last decades has shipped a tremendous amount of its manufacturing overseas, mostly to China. This has been due to political corruption and business corruption of our leaders. Most, if not all, of our trade deals have been destructive for the American workers. As it is now, China produces the majority of our pharmaceuticals this country uses. With the advent of the corona virus and the economic destruction it has already caused, much of our manufacturing jobs will be returned to this country.

The "worship" of the dragon similarly to the worship of the beast is not a religious worship. This dragon is not Satan. The "dragon" is a reference to the collective rebellious nature in us. We, the people, give authority to the beast when we elect our leaders. The secular progressive mindset that is against God lives in this dragon. The dragon is in our nature.

*"The beast was given a mouth to utter proud words and blas-phemies and to exercise its authority for forty-two months." —
Revelation 13:5 (NIV)*

This is an interesting prophecy. Other than an overlap and redundancy of these prophecies, they are also not lineal, which means this prophecy seems to not be in sequence to the verse before it and after it but rather a standalone prophecy.

The first beast with the ten horns, is the United States, as is the next beast with the two horns. It just identifies the follow-on administration. More about that in verse 11.

The first beast was during the Obama administration, but verses 1 through 10 seem to cover a period of time covering both the Obama and the Trump administrations. This verse does not seem to fit the Obama administrations. The forty-two months are giving us an important clue. It does not support the seven-year tribulation, and this has nothing to do with the tribulation. This time frame gives us evidence of an event which is about to happen.

"It opened its mouth to blaspheme God, and to slander his name and his dwelling place and those who live in heaven." — Revelation 13:6 (NIV)

If these first ten verses are not lineal and cover both administrations, then this prophecy has already been fulfilled. It is my belief that President Obama put himself above all that is "called god" when he pushed homosexual marriage into law (2nd Thessalonians 2:4). To side track a bit here, this verse in Thessalonians has an interesting vernacular, "all that is called god." This is describing the institutional church. The body of Christ is not an organization. The remnant may attend organized church, but the organizations themselves are not "God." They are those that are called god. They live in man's truth. The leaders of these organizations are the ones claiming to be messiah. Jesus told us about them. This does not disparage the body of Christ, the invisible church or the remnant.

Obama was not in support of sound doctrine, nor did he support institutional church doctrine. We can see his slander against God from a town hall in 2008:

"And it's not surprising then they get bitter, they cling to guns or religion or antipathy toward people who aren't like them or anti-immigrant sentiment or anti-trade sentiment as a way to explain their frustrations."

"It was given power to wage war against God's holy people and to conquer them. And it was given authority over every tribe, people, language and nation." — Revelation 13:7 (NIV)

Under the Obama administration, war had indeed been waged on God's people. The "woke" culture, which he endorses greatly, accelerated under his administration. The culture continues even to this day. Trump does not support it; in fact, he fights against it. In the prior administration, believers were forced to do things against their beliefs, perform job duties against their consciences or lose their business, which many of them chose instead of compromising their beliefs.

"All inhabitants of the earth will worship the beast—all whose names have not been written in the Lamb's book of life, the Lamb who was slain from the creation of the world." — Revelation 13:8 (NIV)

This is another incredible verse. If we understand this verse, everything falls into place, everything;

Job 38:21, Ephesians 1:4 and Jeremiah 1:5

None of us had our names written in the book of life before the foundation of the planet! This category of people is us. Our rebellion against God happened before the foundation of the planet which is why we are here. Those who did not rebel stayed with God. They are the ones who had their names written in the book of life before the foundation of the planet. Read Ephesians 1:4.

Again, this is not about religious worship. "Worship the beast" is a reference to the United States' predominance on this planet as an economic and military powerhouse. Those in opposition to us militarily or economically do not prosper. The entire planets economy revolves around the United States, which is why we hold the world's reserve currency.

"Whoever has ears, let them hear. 10 'If anyone is to go into captivity, into captivity they will go. If anyone is to be killed with the sword, with the sword they will be killed.' This calls for patient endurance and faithfulness on the part of God's people." – *Revelation 13:9–10 (NIV)*

The placement of this passage in the Bible gives us its meaning. Today, there is a great divide in this country; in fact, God describes us as a "deeply divided nation." In this divide, ideology seem to be the catalyst of much hate. The divide seems to be very well defined along religious and social issues. This divide has pitted one against the other. The extent of it goes far beyond what anyone could have imagined just a few decades ago. The attempted overthrow of the Government by a very corrupt presidential administration, one in which our law enforcement and intel agencies acted lawlessly to achieve an objective. This lawlessness is just an indication of this spiritual war which is raging in this country. We are seeing the war play out in the corrupt main stream media; we see it play out on social media, and we see it play out in our places of employments.

In this war, ideologies are weaponized to an extent of people losing their employment, their careers, their reputations and even their freedom for having the wrong opinions. In this war, if you are identified on the wrong side of the "woke" culture, you will be persecuted. This verse is telling us about today's dynamic. It also implies to stay out of the fight. "This calls for the endurance and faithfulness of the saints." If it does not imply us staying out of the fight, it certainly is telling us we will be attacked for it. It does not tell us to deny God or deny our beliefs. We should never compromise our faith. The secular war waging now cannot be won. It will not be, not before the return of Christ. If this were the case, God would not have promised to protect us by isolating us in the end days and there would be no need of a rapture. This planet is about to destroy itself; the sequence of events that God told us about through the prophecies has started.

"Then I saw a second beast, coming out of the earth. It had two horns like a lamb, but it spoke like a dragon." — Revelation 13:11 (NIV)

There is a time overlap with this verse because Apostle John previously said the wound was healed. At this point, the wound has not yet happened. Again, the beast is the United States. The two horns are a presidential administration. It is unclear which one it is. My initial thought was it was the Trump administration, but I believe him to be a man of faith. The current administration, the man speaking like a dragon is a man speaking with the nature of a man.

The beast is the same beast with just a different head (different leadership).

Both Trump and Pence have professed their faith in God. They are surrounded by church leaders.

Revelation 13:12 "It exercised all the authority of the first beast on its behalf, and made the earth and its inhabitants worship the first beast, whose fatal wound had been healed." (NIV)

The fatal wound is clear. It will be an economic collapse of an extent not seen since the great depression. One of our Presidential administrations will "set up an image" to the beast and will "deceive" the nations. I explained this in the previous book. The prophecy means this nation will default on its staggering debt, of which many nations own. Setting up an image of the beast, as so it will talk, means we will shift from our current fiat economy into an electronic (Crypto) currency. I thought this would happen under the Trump administration. It may still. I believe Trump will be back in office at some point. Chapter 15, Time, Times and a half a time explains this.

"And it performed great signs, even causing fire to come down from heaven to the earth in full view of the people." — Revelation 13:13 (NIV)

This is a military reference. It seems to happen here after the "head being wounded." It "performed" could be a future tense or past tense; it really doesn't matter. The reference is that this man will have the authority to command a military action. Trump has done this already. He most likely will regain office as commander-in-chief. This prophecy could be fulfilled in the future or defined in the past when he ordered the strike in Iran. I strongly suspect it is a future military action taken against China. We may not know until it happens. I also believe China will be responsible for the attack on New York City, which has yet to happen. If the attack is before or after the economic collapse is unknown. I believe they are related.

"Because of the signs it was given power to perform on behalf of the first beast, it deceived the inhabitants of the earth. It ordered

them to set up an image in honor of the beast who was wounded by the sword and yet lived." — Revelation 13:14 (NIV)

This is an incredibly powerful prophecy. There is so much information about economic developments in this verse. Those who are paying attention should really listen. In an earlier verse, it states:

"Blessed is the one who reads aloud the words of this prophecy, and blessed are those who hear it and take to heart what is written in it, because the time is near." — Revelation 1:3 (NIV)

This is not a "spiritual" blessing. It's another type of blessing. One that one would get in order to prepare.

Listen.

The deception is not a spiritual deception. It has an entirely different meaning. The deception is in our bond market. The deception is in the value of empty promises. When the bond market defaults, either this country will directly default on its promise or the dollar will be worthless. There is support in another prophecy:

"Two pounds of wheat for a day's wages, and six pounds of barley for a day's wages, and do not damage the oil and the wine!" — Revelation 6:6 (NIV)

Our money will be mostly worthless; that will be the deception, and it will be the impetus to shift from our fiat-based currency to that other currency. If the first part of this verse speaks to inflation, which it does, the second part of this verse, "do not damage the oil and the wine," is telling us something else. Something very important about this economic collapse. Something Isaiah said.

"it will be the same for priest as for people, for the master as for his servant, for the mistress as for her servant, for seller as for buyer,

for borrower as for lender, for debtor as for creditor." — Isaiah 24:2 (NIV)

Isaiah put an emphasis on concept of "borrower and lender." Wealthy people seem to fare well in this collapse. Why? What do wealthy people have that the poor or middle class don't have? Their debt is less than their assets. They will be able to protect themselves in this crash. If there is a reset, the lender may be punished, but the borrower will be punished more. Gone may be the days when bankruptcy will protect irresponsibility. In this new system, people will not be able to run from their reckless debt and keep their assets. I believe the new system will wipe out those underwater financially. Now would be a good time to be debt-free.

"The second beast was given power to give breath to the image of the first beast, so that the image could speak and cause all who refused to worship the image to be killed." — Revelation 13:15 (NIV)

The "image" of the beast is our currency. The "breath to the image" and "so it could speak" mean our currency will transition from the paper fiat currency to one which takes the form of an electronic currency. The "speaks" is a reference to our currency being controlled by our technology. This is the shift. It will become necessary due to the reckless spending by our corrupt government. They will have no choice. This country will never be able to honor its' debt. That is the deception. That is what *"it deceived the inhabitants of the earth"* means. Those on this planet holding our treasuries are in for a rude awakening. Again, the worship is not a religious worship. Those not abiding by the "new" currency will not be able to function under the new system. If believers identify this as the "mark" and refuse it, they will be making a mistake. These prophecies were never meant as a litmus test. That is what the current established doctrine is telling us. The IC is not correct. The new currency will be the mark of the beast. Believers will willingly receive it as will everyone else on the planet.

"It also forced all people, great and small, rich and poor, free and slave, to receive a mark on their right hands or on their foreheads, 17 so that they could not buy or sell unless they had the mark, which is the name of the beast or the number of its name. 18 This calls for wisdom. Let the person who has insight calculate the number of the beast, for it is the number of a man. That number is 666." — Revelation 13:16 (NIV)

The system for the mark is already here; we have for the most part all taken it. "Forcing" people to take it isn't a litmus test for believers. We will be forced to use technology to use this currency.

The number has been calculated; no one is listening. We are the ones not having our names written in the book of life before the foundation of the planet. We have already taken or will take the mark. At some point, once the currency shifts to an electronic currency, a crypto currency, we will need devices to transact business, any business. From buying a cup of coffee to buying a house, the currency will be electronic. The end of paper currency. We will all take the mark of the beast, or you will not be able to function in our society. You will not be able to buy food, medicine, cigars or anything. All business will be transacted via devices. We will all take the mark, even those who have not taken it yet.

Our phones will be able to make these transactions. They do already for people using this technology. It won't be a choice in the future. It is not a litmus test for believers. In *Cursed Above all Cattle*, we go into great detail of this.

For many generations, the IC has taught this verse in a certain way. It's false. The narrative on this verse was derived from the violation of Daniel 8:26, 12:4 and 12:9. It will not be a litmus test for believers. You will not be able to function without it.

This prophecy is one of identification and time reference. It identifies who we are, those whose names were not written in the book of life before the foundation of the Earth, and of time. It puts us in the end days of these prophecies. The institutional church is misleading its' members.

The 666 is very simple. It is a representation of the technology needed not only for the new currency, but it is needed to buy and sell anything now. It is a reference to the World Wide Web.

To be clear, the World Wide Web, the new electronic currency, our current technology, the internet and the way we communicate with one another is all part of the same thing. The 666 is a reference to WWW. They are part of the thing we cannot buy or sell without. They are all a part of this "mark."

CHAPTER 13:

Secret of the Nephilim

"The sons of God saw that the daughters of humans were beautiful, and they married any of them they chose. 3 Then the LORD said, 'My Spirit will not contend with humans forever, for they are mortal; their days will be a hundred and twenty years.' 4 The Nephilim were on the earth in those days — and also afterward — when the sons of God went to the daughters of humans and had children by them. They were the heroes of old, men of renown." — Genesis 6:2-4 (NIV)

Why did God wipe out the planet in the time of Noah? What is Leviathan? Who are the 144,000? Who are the Nephilim?

They are all related. Once we put meaning to what happened during flood, more of the prophecies will be revealed. The 144,000 come from the population of the Nephilim.

There is so much to unwind here. These next two chapters will explain who the 144,000 are and where they came from.

Before we do understand who the Nephilim are, we need to look at something which happened in Genesis 3:

"The LORD God made garments of skin for Adam and his wife and clothed them." — Genesis 3:21 (NIV)

This verse will tie in the Nephilim in Genesis 6, the 144,000 mentioned in Revelation and the angels who lost their authority in Jude 1:6.

Yes, it is a lot to take in.

God making garments for Adam and Eve is not a benign verse. Banter from God. A meaningless statement. God is telling us something. Adam and Eve could not have survived without assistance. The human race could not have survived early on without assistance.

God knew before Adam and Eve were even created, they would disobey and bring "sin into this world." Their sin was born out of their rebellion against God before the foundation of the planet, as was ours.

As the planet was created for us to live in this rebellion, processes also needed to be put in place. Not just for the survival of Adam and Eve, but to ensure the human race existed for a long enough time for Gods plan to be finished. If these processes were not in place, God's plan would not work. If we look at many scriptures, we can see what God's plan has been. It is far from what is taught.

The Nephilim were a part of this plan, we will see that shortly. Before we do, we need to look at a collection of scriptures and put meaning to them. This will help us understand what the processes were about.

The first one comes in Genesis 1;

"God saw all that He did and it was very good." — *Genesis 1:30 (NIV)*

This is a verse of process; it is not a "moral" statement made by God. This process is the one that made life inhabitable for man. An environment had to be put in place that was conducive to sustain our life on this Earth. Not just our life, but the other life on the planet that would sustain us. After all, this Earth was made in order for us to live out our rebellion. Although man has only been on the planet for six-thousand years, the planet itself is much older. In the order of 4.5 billion years old. In the time before Adam and Eve, the dinosaurs roamed the Earth. They would not have been compatible with human life, so God removed them from the planet. Their existence must have had a rational.

We will very briefly speak to some other processes God has put us under. We can speak more in detail in another book, but for now we just need to understand why they are here before we go into detail on the Nephilim.

- God sets up Kings and Kingdoms: God's purpose was to sustain the environment on the planet, keep a balance. If not, man would have destroyed himself long ago. This is not a "moral" process. One in which God sets up righteous men to lead. No at all has this ever been the case. Evil men have ruled the planet from the beginning. Nor was it the intent of this process. It was strictly to control the survival of the human race though a balance of man's power on the planet. It had to continue in order for us to live out our rebellion the last six-thousand years.

- Submit to Government leaders: If we look at this as a moral statement it will seem to conflict with the periods in history when Government leaders did evil things. Did God tell us to submit to Hitler or Stalin? Or any of the other evil dictators who have ruled on this planet? On the surface it seems to be a nonsensical command. If we don't look at this as a process, it will never make sense. The process, as the prior one, was to maintain the balance in which the human race would continue. The process was not to put godly men as our leaders. The planet is and has been in rebellion to God.

• Submit to the Church leaders: Again, this is a verse of process. Jesus told the multitude to do exactly as the Scribes and Pharoses told them, do as they say, not as they do. Has anyone ever asked about this? Jesus was telling them to listen and obey the leaders who rejected Him. Why would He do that? If we don't see this as a process, then we should think Jesus would have told them to reject those who rejected Him. No, this is a process. God uses man's church for His purpose for His plan. Certainly, the parents who had their children molested by Catholic Priest should have an issue with submitting to that Church. If we look at this as a command, or a "moral" statement, and not a process, it will make little sense. This process is different from the first two which were to keep nations in check, submitting to the church I believe was to keep a divine obscuration in place, which was explained in depth in *Cursed Above All Cattle*. God has kept us in the dark as to who we really are, it is the mystery. Our IC does not mention of when the rebellion happened, nor will they teach any verse which makes little sense without the knowledge of it. It should be now lifted.

- In Genesis 6, we read about the "sons of God." They are the Nephilim. God put them on this planet for a purpose. They had a function, the same one we read about in Genesis 3:21. They were needed to assist and guide man. Not to interfere with man's rebellion or change the trajectory, but control the environment in which man could live out his rebellion. To be clear, man has always had the ability to repent. Then and now. It is why we are on the planet. God has always wanted us back.

The Nephilim had this function. A fine balance of controlling the environment while at the same time, allowing man to repent. If they had not been on the planet at this time, because of our natures, man would have destroyed himself before the population and civilizations would sustain itself. That was their function.

But something unexpected happened. Something God had not planned on. Some of the Nephilim did something they should not have done. The Bible tells us this; they intermixed with the human females. The book of Jude mentions something, "angels who lost their authority." That were these Nephilim.

"They could marry any of them they chose," this is a derogatory statement of the female's nature. The Nephilim should not have done this because it set up a disaster.

This is what happened.

Those Nephilim were unlike the humans on the planet. They had flesh and blood, but they were superior to the men on the planet. They were not here to live out their rebellion as we are; God put them here for a function. Having sexual relationships with the human females was not part of the plan. They had offspring, which led to disastrous results. The offspring were the "men of renown." But the offspring were not "sons of God"; they were humans, humans born into the rebellion as we were, except they had superior DNA. That became a problem. It was not the Nephilim who were evil, it was the offspring. They were physically and mentally superior to the others. Because of it they dominated. They lived in rebellion and dominated the environment. That is what allowed them to live in the wickedness, certainly no one could oppose them. Because of their dominance and their rebellion, they were able to congeal the spirit of men against God. This congealment is a function of human nature; it is the nature of tribalism. When the nature congeals against God, this is the Leviathan. It is in our Satan nature, our rebellious nature against God. It was not supposed to congeal at this point in time because it would prevent man from reconciling with God. It was not supposed to happen.

The nature of it even surprised God. We know that because he told us this. God said, "He regretted making man." That is what He was telling us!

Once this Leviathan took hold, there was no going back. The veracity of it, of the rebellion against God, gave our Creator little choice. He had to destroy it.

From Psalm 74;

14 It was you who crushed the heads of Leviathan and gave it as food to the creatures of the desert. 15 It was you who opened up springs and streams; you dried up the ever-flowing rivers. (NIV)

This entire chapter of Psalm 74 is about the flood. The Archaios serpent, the devil, does not give fuel to Leviathan; he doesn't get here until the end. Man's nature fuels Leviathan, our Satan nature.

After the flood, God put mitigations in place:

Then the LORD said, "My Spirit will not contend with humans forever, for they are mortal; their days will be a hundred and twenty years" — Genesis 6:3 (NIV)

This is the first mitigation. The 120 years are a limit on the lifespan of the Nephilim. Since some of them lost their authority, causing God to destroy the planet, God limited their exposure to this life span.

We see another mitigation in the land of Shinar, the Tower of Babel. The congealment was not due to the dominance of the Nephilim's offspring, but may have been just a function of human civilization, one in which may not have any natural competition to keep it in check.

After the flood, we are told of giants. The DNA of the Nephilim survived the flood, no doubt through the wives of Noah's sons. God dealt with them. To prevent the congealment from happening again.

Today, as in the days of Noah, Leviathan is with us. It is raging.

CHAPTER 14:

The 144,000

The book of Revelation tells us about 144,000 servants who will be with us on this planet and receive a seal. Who are they? What is their purpose? We are given a lot of information about them.

"Do not harm the land or the sea or the trees until we put a seal on the foreheads of the servants of our God." — Revelation 7:3 (NIV)

This verse gives us information about the timing of their arrival. It means, they will be here before the destruction, before New York City is destroyed and most likely before Satan gets thrown out of Heaven.

14:3 *"And they sang a new song before the throne and before the four living creatures and the elders. No one could learn the song except the 144,000 who had been redeemed from the earth." (NIV)*

The 144,000 are not who we think. Certainly not what we have been taught. These men were "redeemed from the earth," which means, they were alive at one point and died.

14: 4 "These are those who did not defile themselves with women, for they remained virgins. They follow the Lamb wherever he goes. They were purchased from among mankind and offered as first fruits to God and the Lamb. 5 No lie was found in their mouths; they are blameless." (NIV)

They were virgins; they were blameless; no lie was found in their mouths. On the surface, this seems to conflict with scripture.

"for all have sinned and fall short of the glory of God," — Romans 3:23 (NIV)

To understand who these men are and where they came from, we need to dig much deeper. We start with Genesis. We will find Romans 3 doesn't apply to these men. Why it doesn't apply will be the key to their identity.

"The sons of God saw that the daughters of humans were beautiful, and they married any of them they chose. 3 Then the LORD said, 'My Spirit will not contend with humans forever, for they are mortal; their days will be a hundred and twenty years.' 4 The Nephilim were on the earth in those days — and also afterward — when the sons of God went to the daughters of humans and had children by them. They were the heroes of old, men of renown." — Genesis 6:2–4 (NIV)

Has anyone asked questions to our church leaders about these passages? More paradoxes. More nonsensical answers. More unanswered questions. How could an angel marry a human? Why would God allow it? They are not in the flesh, and if they were, God certainly would have control over them; there is much more to this.

"My spirit will not contend with humans forever"

This verse has profound meaning. We can put meaning to Genesis 6. To understand who the 144,000 are is to understand this passage in Genesis.

Before we do, we need to go back even further in scripture to Genesis 3:21.

"The LORD God made garments of skin for Adam and his wife and clothed them." (NIV)

This verse will tie in the Nephilim in Genesis 6, the 144,000 mentioned in Revelation and the angels who lost their authority in Jude 1:6.

This verse in Genesis is not a benign verse. Banter from God. A meaningless verse. God is telling us something which up to this point has either been ignored or not understood. Adam and Eve could not have survived without assistance. The human race could not have survived early on without assistance.

Humans have been on this planet for six-thousand years. When God put us here, a process needed to be put in place for our survival. Not just our survival but a process in which man would be able to continue in the plan God put in place.

The first indication of this plan was given to us in Genesis 1:30. "God saw all that He did and it was very good." That was a verse of process. The process was that the environment which God put in place was conducive to sustain our life on this Earth. After all this, Earth was made in order for us to live out our rebellion. Although man has only been on the planet for six-thousand years, the planet itself is much older. In the order of 4.5 billion years old. In that time, before Adam and Eve, is when the dinosaurs roamed the Earth. They would not have been compatible with human life so God removed them from the planet. Their existence in of itself had rational.

Before we examine how Genesis 3:21 ties into those other passages, we need to understand something. We are on this planet because we rebelled against God. That is the reason we are here. God has allowed us, in fact built the environment for us to live out an existence apart from Him. He has very little influence over us. He has exerted the control and authority on this planet to the extent needed to sustain us. Yes, God does hear us and answer prayer. Yes, we can reconcile with God and walk in faith. It still does not alleviate the fact we live in rebellion. Satan does not have control or authority of us. He has been in the spiritual realm since the beginning. He accuses us day and night but he will not be on the planet until the end days. God has been with us from the beginning ensuring the planet continues.

Allowing us to live in our rebellion is why God does not directly show His existence to us. It is why the angels are hidden from us. God could at any moment stop this planet and end the rebellion. Stop the pain. He does not because we asked for this. He is allowing us to live out our rebellion without influence from Satan or Himself. He does need to intervene. Not to stop our rebellion but to sustain the planet.

Genesis 3:21 is a mention of something. Man needed assistance from the beginning, or the race would have never survived. If it did survive, it may have taken a direction God did not want it to take. Indeed, it did. God said He regretted making man. A regret is something which only happens if you either make a mistake or something does not go as you have planned. Something did go wrong. God had to do a reset on the planet because of it. The wickedness which happened on the planet was not due to Satan. It was due to man's nature. The natures of man congealed. The society before the flood became homogenous. Because of that tribalism took a great hold. It's much like today. Tribalism has gripped this planet. The great divide in this nation and in the world is due to it. This was not supposed to happen back in the beginning. That congealing of the human spirit happened again after the flood. God stopped it. It is what really happened in the land of Shinar (the Tower of Babel). God would not allow the congealing of the spirit. It was too soon. It would have thrown off the process. We needed to be allowed to continue. Today the congealing is happening again. This time God will not stop it. Our time is up.

The assistance God gave mankind did not stop in the Garden. Not at all. In the beginning, God needed a physical presence on this planet without throwing off the purpose for us to be here. That is what Genesis 6 is telling us. The assistance came in the form of the "sons of God," angels living with us on the planet. They were put here to serve a function. They were the Nephilim. They were here before and after the flood. God had rational for their existence.

God said, "My spirit cannot contend with these humans forever," then mentioned: their days will be limited to one hundred and twenty years. The institutional church has this all wrong. The 120 years wasn't about the mortals. The 120 years was about the Nephilim. They lived only 120 years. God put a limit on them because "my spirit cannot contend . . ." This life span has a direct tie to the 144,000.

In Revelation 14:3, it tells us something about these Nephilim.

". . . except the 144,000 who had been redeemed from the earth."

The 144,000 had been alive at one point; they died and then were redeemed from the Earth. The 144,000 came from the Nephilim. We will find not all the Nephilim made the cut.

There is much more about them we need to understand. Not all of them abided by God's wishes.

These sons of God, the Nephilim, the population from which the 144,00 will come from are not like us. We are here because we rebelled against God before the foundation of the planet. The Nephilim did not. They were not here due to a rebellion prior to the foundation of the planet. God put them on the planet to ensure the survival and the direction of man. Before the flood, we are told the sons of God interacted with the females on the planet. That should not have happened. We will read about these angels in the book of Jude.

The 144,000 were taken from this population of the Nephilim. They, however, did not interact with the females. We know this because the Bible tells us so:

14: 4 "These are those who did not defile themselves with women, for they remained virgins. They follow the Lamb wherever he goes. They were purchased from among mankind and offered as first fruits to God and the Lamb. 5 No lie was found in their mouths; they are blameless." (NIV)

These 144,000 are from the Nephilim. They did not rebel against God. That is why they are "blameless."

They are not "blameless" due to their redemption like the multitudes which had their robes "washed in the blood of the Lamb." That was an entirely different category of people. The Bible makes no reference to the 144,000 receiving salvation. Redeemed from the

Earth is strictly speaking to them coming back to life (in the flesh). We will cover them before we finish this chapter.

"...did not defile themselves with women, for they remained virgins."

This is not a statement of morality. If it were, then it would tell us we defile ourselves with women when we have sexual relationships with them. Or it would be telling us women are defiled. This passage is telling us these men were not put on the planet because they rejected and rebelled against God. They were put on this planet because God had a purpose for them. The Nephilim that "defiled" themselves with women will pay a price for it.

These Nephilim, from which the 144,000 came from, had human bodies. We know this because the Bible tells us where they came from. They were born into the twelve tribes. They were human, but they did not rebel against God. They had human parents which will distinguish them from Christ who did not have a human father. We are told some of them sinned.

Since the 144,000 is an exact number of 12,000 from each tribe, the population would have been much bigger. Obviously, those Nephilim who interacted with the human females will not be part of the 144,000. Most likely nor will some of the others, since it is that exact number.

We were told about the sons of God, the Nephilim, who interacted with the human females;

"And the angels who did not keep their positions of authority but abandoned their proper dwelling—these he has kept in darkness, bound with everlasting chains for judgment on the great Day."—Jude 1:6 (NIV)

Those Nephilim who had sexual relationships with the human females are these angels who did not keep their positions of authority. Remember, these men were "blameless" but were not born of Immaculate Conception. They had human parents. Even though they were not born into sin, they fell to the temptation of the beautiful females.

We need to look at one more passage before we complete this chapter;

14:9 *"After this I looked, and there before me was a great multitude that no one could count, from every nation, tribe, people and language, standing before the throne and before the Lamb. They were wearing white robes and were holding palm branches in their hands. 10 And they cried out in a loud voice: 'Salvation belongs to our God, who sits on the throne, and to the Lamb.' 11 All the angels were standing around the throne and around the elders and the four living creatures. They fell down on their faces before the throne and worshiped God, 12 saying: 'Amen! Praise and glory and wisdom and thanks and honor and power and strength be to our God for ever and ever. Amen!' 13 Then one of the elders asked me, 'These in white robes—who are they, and where did they come from?' 14 I answered, 'Sir, you know.' And he said, 'These are they who have come out of the great tribulation; they have washed their robes and made them white in the blood of the Lamb.' 15 Therefore, 'they are before the throne of God and serve him day and night in his temple; and he who sits on the throne will shelter them with his presence.' 16 'Never again will they hunger; never again will they thirst. The sun will not beat down on them,' nor any scorching heat. 17 For the Lamb at the center of the throne will be their shepherd; 'he will lead them to springs of living water.' 'And God will wipe away every tear from their eyes.'"* (NIV)

This passage gives us an enormous amount of information. Much of it will conflict with established doctrine.

These men are not the 144,000, nor do they come from a seven-year tribulation. That is what it is telling us in verse 9, no one could count. We can count 144,000 as well as we can count the number who will reconcile with God the last seven years on this planet. These men and women are the ones who have lived over the history of this planet and had reconciled with God. We know they lived in their rebellion at one point; we are told this in verse 14. Their robes were washed in the blood of the lamb. They couldn't have their robes washed unless they had rebelled.

They came from the great tribulation. Living in the rebellion to God is the great tribulation. It's been going on now for six-thousand years. There is no seven-year tribulation. That is a mythical false narrative from the institutional church. It has no basis in the Bible. The seventy weeks of Daniel does not support it. When Jesus mentioned the end day tribulation, it was not a "new" tribulation. What Jesus was telling us was that things will get really bad near the end. Most likely when Satan gets thrown out of Heaven.

CHAPTER 15:

Time, Times and Half a Time

Three times God told Daniel the prophecies that were given to him were sealed up until the end days. Three times. In the complete arrogance of man, the institutional church attempted to unseal them before they were allowed to. In doing so, they have formed countless false narratives. These narratives have had an unfortunate effect on those who belong to an institutional church. They have been led astray as Jesus told us they would be. Because of the false narratives many believers are looking for something which will never happen.

Three times in the Bible, a certain phrase is used. Daniel 7:25, "time, times and half a time" Daniel 12:7, ". . . time, times and half a time," and again in Revelation 12:14, "time, times and half a time."

The institutional church tells us this is a three-and-a-half-year period. This is absolutely false. This phrase actually has a profound meaning and knowledge which has been given to us to be used by us.

"The ten horns are ten kings who will come from this kingdom. After them another king will arise, different from the earlier ones; he will subdue three kings. 25 He will speak against the Most High and oppress his holy people and try to change the set times and the laws. The holy people will be delivered into his hands for a time, times and half a time." — Daniel 7:24 (NIV)

We have gone into great depth in the previous book identifying who this "diverse king" was, the king different than the ones before him. I believe this king was Barack Obama; it could be no other. The ten kings and the three kings were explained as well. The phrase time, times and a half a time is significant, and it is not a three and a half year period of time.

In this instance, in this verse the time, times and half a time has a very negative connotation. The term itself refers to a presidential term in office. I believe the first "time" is one term, second term, "times" is the reelection and the second term in office and the "half a time" is the influence an ex-president maintains. The negative connotation in this verse is a reflection of a man who weaponized the law enforcement agencies and intel communities in order to maintain power for his ideology. We are told this in the book of 2nd Thessalonians 2.

3 "Don't let anyone deceive you in any way, for that day will not come until the rebellion occurs and the man of lawlessness is revealed, the man doomed to destruction. 4 He will oppose and will exalt himself over everything that is called God or is worshiped, so that he sets himself up in God's temple, proclaiming himself to be God." (NIV)

Barack Obama set himself at odds with the institutional church when he endorsed and forced gay marriage into law. He disparaged believers. I believe his administration weaponized and corrupted law enforcement and intelligence agencies to suit his own agenda. That would prove him to be that lawless man. Putting himself above all that is "called God" means he overrode the institutional church.

Just to be clear. Christians, born again believers or those that walk in faith are the body of Christ. They may or may not belong to an organization. The organizations themselves, the institutional churches are *not* the body of Christ. They are businesses whose leaders are leading the planet away from God's truth. Today's organizational church is in large part the Laodicean church. It is what Thessalonians refers to as "all that is called God."

The term "time, times, and half a time" will become relevant in Revelation 12.

We are in the end days, and the prophecies are now unsealed. We can now put meaning to the "the time, times and half a time."

"The man clothed in linen, who was above the waters of the river, lifted his right hand and his left hand toward heaven, and I heard him swear by him who lives forever, saying, 'It will be for a time, times and half a time. When the power of the holy people has been finally broken, all these things will be completed.'" — Daniel 12:7 (NIV)

The first election of Barack Obama could have been considered a mistake. By the second election, he was no mystery. I believe Barack Obama did more damage to this country than any other man before him. He progressed his secular progressive agenda at the expense of established law, of which he had no restriction in violating. He used racial division and class warfare, identity politics and deception to control the electorate. This country elected him to a second term.

This country has murdered seventy-two million unborn babies. It is beyond reprehensible. It is ungodly, immoral and repugnant. It is lawful in this country for same sex couples to legally marry. This is directly against God's Commandments. This country has ungodliness in it. The power of the holy people being broken is a reflection of the loss of influence the Christians have over this country. This prophecy was fulfilled. Again, the time, times and half a time is a reflection of his two terms in office. A negative connotation.

"The woman was given the two wings of a great eagle, so that she might fly to the place prepared for her in the wilderness, where she would be taken care of for a time, times and half a time, out of the serpent's reach." — Revelation 12: 14 (NIV)

The same phrase repeated but this time it is in a positive connotation. The meaning is the same but it is just a different administration. I believe this prophecy means Donald Trump will serve two terms in office. Either way, the "time, times and half a time" is not a three and a half year time period, it is a reference to an election cycle.

We have seen the other prophecies referencing President Trump. In chapter five, the antichrist was revealed. The false narratives by the IC to support a false narrative of the antichrist was revealed. Trump was put in office by God. If the correct interpretation of the "time, times and a half a time" is correct, in that it means two presidential terms; it would mean Trump will, one way or the other, return to office. As unlikely as it seems at the current time, I believe Trump will be back in office. Not to "turn the country around" or in support of an ideology supported by God, remember, Barack Obama put himself above "all that is called God," which is the institutional church. God does not care about our ideology nor is he rooting for a side. We are all broken to the same level. This country certainly has evil in it. The clay. God is not pulling for the iron to overcome and promote the IC. Everything is in accordance with His plan. Our politics, our country and our ideologies are of no concern to God.

Our religious leaders are in violation of God's Commandments and are in violation of the restrictions in Daniel. They put one man (themselves) above another. They claim to speak for God. They are what is "called God." We are broken, and God does not support our country. That is in our doctrine only. It's false.

One last note on the "times, time and half a time." The IC has used this term to defend a doctrine about a "seven-year tribulation. They say the phase represents three and a half years. Both together, therefore, represent seven years. This is false. There is no seven-year tribulation. There never has been. This planet has been in tribulation since the beginning. The "great" tribulation Jesus was talking about does not have a time associated with it. It's the same tribulation that we have been in for six-thousand years, except only worse. I suspect the "great" begins when Satan gets thrown out of Heaven.

CHAPTER 16:

The Seven Bowls

"Then I heard a loud voice from the temple saying to the seven angels, "Go, pour out the seven bowls of God's wrath on the earth." 2 The first angel went and poured out his bowl on the land, and ugly, festering sores broke out on the people who had the mark of the beast and worshiped its image." —Revelation 16:1 (NIV)

We have all taken or will the mark of the beast. We are the ones who did not have our names written in the book of life before the foundation of the planet. This verse is a curse, not for failing the false litmus test. It's a curse for the people on the planet. It's a time reference, not a test. The technology existing today which will allow us to conduct all financial transactions electronically will be a requirement.

This is our curse. How big this land is could be anywhere between sixteen hundred stadia or the entire planet. The timing of this is up for conjecture, and its time relevance is modern current day, we know this because the mark of the beast happens in the end times. Our time.

The sores are a reference to radiation poisoning. The land could be the result of New York City being destroyed by a nuclear weapon, which will happen. It could be a reference to the larger scale world-wide nuclear exchange as well. That will also happen. "All the mountains will shake."

"The second angel poured out his bowl on the sea, and it turned into blood like that of a dead person, and every living thing in the sea died." — Revelation 16:3 (NIV)

With a very large nuclear exchange on this planet, which will happen, the radiative fallout will kill the oceans. Whether the "sea" is a local reference, or a more global reference is again up for debate. But if we put this verse into perspective of other prophesies, we may be able to come up with a conclusion to the size and the scope of it. These are late day prophecies. The implication is that it is a very extensive poisoning of the world's oceans. If this isn't post rapture, the next bowl certainly is.

"The third angel poured out his bowl on the rivers and springs of water, and they became blood. 5 Then I heard the angel in charge of the waters say: 'You are just in these judgments, O Holy One, you who are and who were; 6 for they have shed the blood of your holy people and your prophets, and you have given them blood to drink as they deserve.' 7 And I heard the altar respond: 'Yes, Lord God Almighty, true and just are your judgments.'" — Revelation 16:4 (NIV)

All these judgments are devastating events. Man caused this. In the history of this planet, man has lived in rebellion against God.

Do we think things have improved? We've been told things like there is this thing called the indomitable human spirit. It's an implication that the human race is inherently good and constantly strives to improve. Achieve enlightenment. The human race progresses. After all, our current woke culture has told us they are attaining this enlightenment through inclusiveness and tolerance. Any believer can tell you this is a profound lie. The secular progressives have not achieved any improvement to the human race, the opposite is true. The woke culture is the preponderance of the rebellion against God. If man had this indomitable human spirit, if man was inherently good and strived for harmony, why would the world be in the current condition? Nothing has changed from the beginning. Man has not improved throughout the generations. If anything, the advances in technology has exaggerated the evil in our nature. It has also allowed the congealing of the human spirit within the rules of tribalism.

With the entire world being linked with instant communication through our advanced technology, we have greatly denigrated into the collection of evil within our societies. Our planet has not improved because we still live in our rebellion.

If the second bowl took out the oceans, which will be devastating enough, this third bowl will take out our fresh water supply. This will really have a devastating impact. Having the water supply gone, the thing life depends on, large populations will die. The death will be from both dehydration as well as radiation poisoning. The only event which would be possible to devastate the oceans and then the fresh water will be nuclear exchanges. We know New York City will be destroyed by a nuclear device. The event in New York could fulfill the prophecy in the first two verses of this chapter. As time goes forward after New York is destroyed, things get progressively worse.

God will have raptured His people prior to this prophecy.

Satan will be on the Earth at this time, him and his angels.

"The fourth angel poured out his bowl on the sun, and the sun was allowed to scorch people with fire. 9 They were seared by the intense heat and they cursed the name of God, who had control over these plagues, but they refused to repent and glorify him." —Revelation 16:8 (NIV)

This gives us a little indication of the size of the nuclear worldwide exchange. Our ozone, as it turns out, is very important for our protection. God's design was beyond our understanding. This design, our ozone layer, will be destroyed by the amount of contamination due to the amount of nuclear devastation.

"The fifth angel poured out his bowl on the throne of the beast, and its kingdom was plunged into darkness. People gnawed their tongues in agony 11 and cursed the God of heaven because of their pains and their sores, but they refused to repent of what they had done." —Revelation 16:10 (NIV)

Again, this is due to the aftermath of the nuclear devastation. It's remarkable that after all this, there will be those remaining on the planet, after the rapture, who will still not repent. It is a remarkable thing, the saints got impatient with God, but He told them to hold off on their impatience. God knows what he is doing. He has given everyone the chance to repent. The amount of this we will never know. It is why things are taking so long. After every chance, after the last one has reconciled, the remainder will pay for their rebellion and lack of reconciliation with God.

"The sixth angel poured out his bowl on the great river Euphrates, and its water was dried up to prepare the way for the kings from the East. 13 Then I saw three impure spirits that looked like frogs; they came out of the mouth of the dragon, out of the mouth of the beast and out of the mouth of the false prophet. 14 They are demonic spirits that perform signs, and they go out to the kings of

the whole world, to gather them for the battle on the great day of God Almighty. 15 'Look, I come like a thief! Blessed is the one who stays awake and remains clothed, so as not to go naked and be shamefully exposed.'" — Revelation 16:12 (NIV)

In Revelation 12:9 Satan and his angels were thrown out of Heaven. Post rapture and with Satan on this planet, those left will be the ones in opposition to God.

"Then they gathered the kings together to the place that in Hebrew is called Armageddon. 17 The seventh angel poured out his bowl into the air, and out of the temple came a loud voice from the throne, saying, 'It is done!'" — Revelation 16:16 (NIV)

The thousand-year reign starts.

CHAPTER 17:

Mystery Babylon

God gave us prophecies. We can understand them. Meaning can be put to them. The meaning will not come from our leaders; they are blinding us to them. The false narratives they have promulgated over the generations have led everyone astray as Jesus told us they would. Through the violations of Daniel, false narratives have been taught and believed. Because we have been blinded and are looking for events which will never occur, we are not seeing the prophecies as they unfold. While it was great for selling books, CDs and movies, the information we have gotten has been false. It has blinded us. Mystery Babylon can now be understood.

Before we decipher this chapter, we need to revisit something. This country has many Christian denominations. There are people who belong to God in each one of these church buildings. Some may even have leaders who are true believers. The people in these churches, the believers, may not be readily apparent. They may not have status or hold positions in these churches. Most likely they won't. Those drawn to such positions may be doing so for other reasons than worshiping God. Most of these believers may remain quiet about their inherent disagreement to the doctrine that they are being taught. They know something is wrong but under the obscuration do not fully understand the depth to it. At the beginning of Revelation, we were told about the seven churches. They worshipped differently, and their doctrine differed. They all had their strengths and weaknesses but they had people in them who belonged to God. Faith and repentance are required for reconciliation not knowledge. Today's lukewarm church, the church of Laodicea, has been described as has been the spirit of the antichrist which Apostle John told us about. The leaders of this church tickle their ears, tell myths about God and will be made as fools. They say Lord, Lord but Jesus said I don't know you. They have led the planet astray, but yet there are those who still belong to God in these places. They reconciled with God through Christ.

The body of Christ are those who belong to God. The body of Christ are not their organizations. In many cases, may not even be their leadership; Jesus told us this.

Understanding this, we can start with who the great prostitute is.

"One of the seven angels who had the seven bowls came and said to me, "Come, I will show you the punishment of the great prostitute, who sits by many waters. 2 With her the kings of the earth committed adultery, and the inhabitants of the earth were intoxicated with the wine of her adulteries." — Revelation 17:1 (NIV)

We start out in this chapter with the prostitute. We will see her punishment in a few verses. The prostitute is not a Christian denomination; it can't be because even the worst Christian churches may have the body of Christ living in them. Reference the seven churches. No, this prostitute is a non-Christian religion. A prostitute for God. It is the Islam faith. It's described to us in verse one and two. "Sits by many waters" means it has a global presence.

"The kings of the earth committed adultery" tell us the influence this religion has on the planet. Fifty-six of the 193-member countries of the United Nations are Islamic states. The Islamic faith is at war with the Christian faith. It has been for thousands of years and yet they seem to be giving a deference not afforded to Christians.

Many people in the world have replaced God with this false religion. It is the prostitute.

"Then the angel carried me away in the Spirit into a wilderness. There I saw a woman sitting on a scarlet beast that was covered with blasphemous names and had seven heads and ten horns. 4 The woman was dressed in purple and scarlet, and was glittering with gold, precious stones and pearls." — Revelation 17:3 (NIV)

This entire verse can now be understood. Meaning can be put to the woman and the beast. In a prior chapter, we identified the beast with the seven heads and ten horns. It is the United States, the deeply divided nation in the book of Daniel. The beast is us. The woman is a city. It sits on the beast. It sits on the United States. This city is New York City. It will be destroyed; we will see that in the next chapter. There is so much that the Bible tells us about this city. The description is certainly not limited to this verse and we will cover much of it in this chapter and the next.

We start here with how it is described, "Glittering with gold, precious stones and pearls." It is a city which holds status, prestige and importance. This is no ordinary city. It is a city of world renown.

"She held a golden cup in her hand, filled with abominable things and the filth of her adulteries. 5 The name written on her forehead was a mystery: BABYLON THE GREAT THE MOTHER OF PROSTITUTES AND OF THE ABOMINATIONS OF THE EARTH." (NIV)

Here is a major clue to who this woman is. This is a direct connection, a direct way we can identify this city. The woman is New York City as represented by the Statue of Liberty. The inscription on the woman, "BABYLON THE GREAT THE MOTHER OF PROSTITUTES AND OF THE ABOMINATIONS OF THE EARTH." This inscription can be interpreted. Meaning can be put to it. It is the inscription engraved onto a plaque representing the Statue.

"Give me your tired, your poor, your huddled masses yearning to breathe free, the wretched refuse of your teeming shore. Send these, the homeless, tempest-tossed to me, I lift my lamp beside the golden door!"

The United States is the beast. Yes, the body of Christ lives among us, but this country is the beast. This nation which celebrates gay marriage, this country which has murdered over seventy-two million babies is not a godly nation.

It may be very difficult for many to come to terms with this. There is a great resistance to see the truth. We are raised to respect the flag. Our parents taught us pride and patriotism for our country. We look at the good and ignore the evil; we are led to believe we are the exceptional nation. Anything other than acknowledgement of this may incur a wrath from the tribalism we live in. If we are seen as unpatriotic because we don't adhere to the rules of patriotism, we may lose status in our tribes, maybe even ousted from the tribe. There is so much evil in our country that we have been conditioned to overlook. The evil is the clay spoken about in the book of Daniel. The Iron is here as well. The iron is us, those who belong to God.

"I saw that the woman was drunk with the blood of God's holy people, the blood of those who bore testimony to Jesus. When I saw her, I was greatly astonished. 7 Then the angel said to me: "Why are you astonished? I will explain to you the mystery of the

woman and of the beast she rides, which has the seven heads and ten horns." — Revelation 17:6 (NIV)

There is little mystery about the ideology of New York City. We need to go no further than to look at the politicians they elect. New York City is a profoundly liberal secular progressive city. They are the clay. Their politicians spew their ungodly nonstop rhetoric against God and God's people. In the name of today's woke culture they profess tolerance and fairness. Nothing could be further from the truth. They show no tolerance for those who profess faith in our Creator.

"The beast, which you saw, once was, now is not, and yet will come up out of the Abyss and go to its destruction. The inhabitants of the earth whose names have not been written in the book of life from the creation of the world will be astonished when they see the beast, because it once was, now is not, and yet will come." — Revelation 17:8 (NIV)

This is an astounding passage. There is so much information given to us in this verse. We can understand it.

Previously in Revelation, Apostle John told us of an angel with his feet on the sea and on the land. There is a very significant connection to this passage.

The beast is the United States, and the woman is New York City. John is not seeing this in a dream; he is seeing it in real time. The angel did not have his feet in two different places; he had his feet in two different times. Apostle John will be here in the flesh if he is not already.

"The beast once was," the beast, the United States, currently holds the world's reserve currency. It is the world's economic power house. It has a financial influence which no country has ever had. It is very much in danger of losing that status at the current time. After decades at the hands of profoundly corrupt leaders in this country we are very much in danger of defaulting on our debt, indeed we will. That is the next piece to this verse. "Now is not", that is a statement Apostle John made in his current time, it's a statement of the present, his present. "now is not", It's not a past statement and it's not a future statement, but it is a present statement. The Apostle John will be here in person when this happens. "Now is not" means Apostle John will be here in the time the United States loses its position of holding the world's reserve currency. This signifies the destruction of the United States' bond market and the end of our fiat currency. It is reflected in other passages, "Two pounds of wheat for a day's wages." There will be massive inflation as the value of our dollar goes down.

"Yet will come up out of the Abyss and then go to it's destruction." We spoke about something in a previous chapter, which directly applies to this verse. "Will come up" means that there will be a shift this country will make away from the fiat currency to an electronic currency. This country will rebound in a very short period of time. The old currency will become worthless, and the new currency will be the currency fueling the recovery of our economic engine. The world indeed will be astonished including our enemies. This will lead to both the destruction of New York City as well as the United States. We will look at what happens to New York City in the next chapter.

"The inhabitants of the earth whose names have not been written in the book of life from the creation of the world." This is a profound statement.

In the prior book, *Cursed Above All Cattle*, we go into great depth on who these people are. It is worth repeating.

We rebelled against God before the foundation of the world.

"For he chose us in him before the creation of the world to be holy and blameless in his sight. In love." — Ephesians 1:4 (NIV)

We see the reference of "those whose names were not written in the book of life before the foundation of the world" on multiple occasions. These people, a category of sorts, are us. It will be very important to realize this going forward. The prophecies will explode open. Anywhere this is mentioned, God is speaking about us. This is not to say we cannot reconcile with God through Christ. It just means we rebelled against God in the beginning. We had our names removed from His book when we did. We did that on our own.

"The inhabitants of the earth whose names have not been written in the book of life . . . will be astonished when they see the beast" (NIV)

This is an important verse. These inhabitants are us. Being astonished means the beast, the United States, the beast with the head wound will recover robustly. Ironically enough, the recovery will lead to our destruction. It will give our enemies the motivation to destroy us as their economies are left in ruin.

It also implies there are inhabitants on the Earth whose names were written in the Book of Life. There are or there will be. The 144,000 who did not defile themselves with women. It's not a sexual restriction as our IC leaders have led us to believe. The reference to "not defiling themselves with women" means that they did not fall with us; they are here for a purpose.

Today's institutional church leaders teach us that there is a dichotomy among these inhabitants. The saved and the unsaved. The "names who have been written in the Book of Life before the foundation of the Earth" are those who have reconciled with God and "those whose names were not" are those who have not reconciled. This is not correct. It's dangerous and may have a devastating impact on the body of Christ if not corrected. First of all, there is a dichotomy, not between the saved and the unsaved, but those on the planet who fell and those who did not. The 144,000 did not fall. They will be here with us on the planet. We touched on this already. It is a dangerous belief. When we are forced to take the mark of the beast, the false doctrine of the dichotomy means the mark is a litmus test for believers. This is not true. Taking the mark is strictly a time reference. Why would God subject us to such a test? The saved will be very hurt if they accept this false teaching.

"This calls for a mind with wisdom. The seven heads are seven hills on which the woman sits. 10 They are also seven kings. Five have fallen, one is, the other has not yet come; but when he does come, he must remain for only a little while. 11 The beast who once was, and now is not, is an eighth king. He belongs to the seven and is going to his destruction. 12 "The ten horns you saw are ten kings who have not yet received a kingdom, but who for one hour will receive authority as kings along with the beast." —Revelation 17:9 (NIV)

There is so much false information about this passage. The seven hills are not Rome. The hills are not physical hills. It's not a geographic reference. The hills can easily be identified by dismissing the false narratives we have been taught by the IC.

The seven heads and ten horns are the United States. The ten horns are a reference to the executive branch and the Supreme Court. Ten individuals with regal authority. The seven heads are a bit more complex. They are more of a historical reference to our nation. These are represented by our seven paper currencies, and yes, the two-dollar bill is still in circulation. These are the heads depicted on our currencies which are past leaders of our nation. In the previous book, *Cursed Above All Cattle*, we go into great depth on this chapter.

On November 30, 2018, George H. W. Bush died. Before his death, there were five ex-presidents still alive and one in office.

"They are also seven kings. Five have fallen, one is . . ." (NIV)

This is giving us an enormous amount of information; it's not all good; in fact, it's very bad. This prophecy was fulfilled after Trump was elected. Five were, one is, one will come for a short time (less than a full term). President Trump was not reelected. The vote of 2020 was massively fraudulent, and Biden won the election. The passage tells us, "He must remain only a short while." This means, Biden will not complete his first term. That may not be much of a stretch; he is obviously severely mentally impaired. It is unlikely he will hold up. Trump, in my understanding of the prophecies, will return to office. The Bible told us this when they said the woman in Revelation 12 would be taken care of for a time, times and a half a time. That meant a two-term presidency as it did in a similar reference in Daniel about President Obama's terms in office. This verse gives us timing of end day events. It is about to be very bad news for this country.

"The ten horns are ten kings who will come from this kingdom. After them another king will arise different from the earlier ones; he will subdue three kings. 25. He will speak against the Most High and oppress his saints and try to change the set times and the laws. The saints will be handed over to him for a time, times and half a time." — Daniel 7:24 (NIV)

"Flee from Babylon! Run for your lives! Do not be destroyed because of her sins. It is time for the Lord's vengeance; He will pay

her what she deserves. Babylon was a gold cup in the Lord's Hand; she made the whole Earth drunk . . ." — Jeremiah 51:6–7 (NIV)

The information this passage gives us is one of timing.

"Kings who have not yet received a kingdom, but who for one hour will receive authority as kings along with the beast." (NIV)

During the Barack Obama administration, there was an all-out war against those of faith. The Supreme Court defied the Constitution as did President Obama when the immorality of gay marriage was made the law of the land. Complete defiance to God's command. They had giving their authority to the beast, the component of the secular progressive ungodly nation. Only one nation on this planet has "kings," individuals with a regal authority, but not have kingdoms. It has to be a description of our political system.

"The beast who once was, and now is not, is an eighth king. He belongs to the seven and is going to his destruction" (NIV)

The horn, the head or the beast can be used interchangeable because it all references the same thing. The leadership of this nation. The beast came from the seven, meaning he came from our political system and was the head of it. He is an eighth king could have two meanings, most likely both. He came from our system and no longer is in authority or he came from our system and still exerts some sort of political influence. Obama does both. This eighth could mean only one of two things at this point. The first is that this king is Obama. He came from the seven and still exerts authority. The second could mean it would be Trump; he came from the seven and exerts authority after he was out of office. In either of these cases, this man will go to destruction.

"They have one purpose and will give their power and authority to the beast. 14 They will wage war against the Lamb, but the Lamb

will triumph over them because he is Lord of lords and King of kings — and with him will be his called, chosen and faithful followers." — Revelation 17:13 (NIV)

Our nation legally kills the unborn. Our nation celebrates gay marriage which is directly against God's commandment. The secular progressive component of our nation controls such things and is not the "iron" which is the population of those living by faith. Contrary to what we are told by our leaders, this is not a godly nation. The godly have not been able to stop the murder of seventy-two million unborn babies. Because of tribalism, patriotism or the thought, our country is an "exceptional" country; we are blinded to these prophecies. Yes, there are born again believers living in this country, people living by faith. It's not the preponderance; if it were, abortion would not be legal. Businesses would not be shut down for refusing to cater to things against their faith and things they believe to be immoral. In order to comply with the false mantra of "tolerance," the believers are treated with intolerance. The entire secular progressive movement in itself is a lie. The white horse pretending to uphold values of acceptance and tolerance, while in reality, they are intolerant and bent on changing fundamental values of those of faith.

"Then the angel said to me, "The waters you saw, where the prostitute sits, are peoples, multitudes, nations and languages. 16 The beast and the ten horns you saw will hate the prostitute. They will bring her to ruin and leave her naked; they will eat her flesh and burn her with fire." — Revelation 17:15 (NIV)

Here the angel tells us what the prostitute is. It's global with different nations and languages. It is Islam, and by its very nature, it is against God. The replacement of God, the prostitute. The Muslim doctrine, Islam, Isis or radical Islam, it does not matter how we describe it, is against God. With a population of 1.8 billion members, they are global and sit on many waters. In the most incredible example of our secular progressive culture, we are told to be tolerant of a religion which is the least tolerant faith on the planet. We are told they are a peaceful religion. Maybe they are when they make up a small amount of the population, but as soon as their numbers grow to a large enough percentage of any nation, they will display how "peaceful" they really are. They will institute Sharia Law and try to subdue any who do not follow the Islam faith.

We are told what will happen to them. Indeed, it has been happening for decades. The beast, the United States, will hate the prostitute and burn her with fire. This country has been burning the prostitute and bringing her to ruin since the war on Isis started decades ago. Since the attack on the World Trade Center, this country has killed Muslims by the hundreds of thousands. This prophecy has been fulfilled as the angel told us.

"For God has put it into their hearts to accomplish his purpose by agreeing to hand over to the beast their royal authority, until God's words are fulfilled. 18 The woman you saw is the great city that rules over the kings of the earth." — Revelation 17:17 (NIV)

Among all the prophecies, there is great redundancy and interconnectivity. The "great city" that rules over the kings of the earth has to be New York City. It is a reference to the United Nations being headquartered in the city. There are many more descriptors for this city. We will see additional descriptors in the next chapter which pinpoint the identity of this woman. Globally, New York City is a key player for worldwide economic activity.

CHAPTER 18

Stand Far Off

"With a mighty voice he shouted: "Fallen! Fallen is Babylon the Great! 'She has become a dwelling for demons and a haunt for every impure spirit, a haunt for every unclean bird, a haunt for every unclean and detestable animal. 3 For all the nations have drunk the maddening wine of her adulteries. The kings of the earth committed adultery with her, and the merchants of the earth grew rich from her excessive luxuries." — Revelation 18:2 (NIV)

God has given us a tremendous amount of information about Mystery Babylon. The prophecies in Jeremiah and in Revelation are not esoteric. It's not useless academic information written just for our curiosity or a benign collection of flowery words. These prophecies have consequences. Real meaning which we can identify. New York City will be destroyed. It will happen. This chapter gives us great detail on how it will happen and even a general geographic location of where the nuclear device will detonate.

Mystery Babylon is New York City. It cannot be any other city on this planet. In *Cursed Above All Cattle*, we went to great lengths to tie the description of New York City to this Mystery Babylon.

If we look at the descriptions given to us, we can see it can be no other city:

- It's a coastal city. "Sea captains will stand far off . . ."
- It has a global presence. "For all nations have drunk the maddening wine of her adulteries."
- The United Nations Headquarters is located in this city. "The woman you saw is the great city that rules over the kings of the earth."

And the final tie;

- "BABYLON THE GREAT THE MOTHER OF PROSTITUTES AND OF THE ABOMINATIONS OF THE EARTH." This inscription ties Mystery Babylon to the inscription on the Statue of Liberty. It could have no other meaning. It will fit no other city on Earth.

The description of Mystery Babylon has to be New York City. It can be no other city. It will be destroyed.

"Terrified at her torment, they will stand far off and cry: 'Woe! Woe, O (to you,) great city, (you) O Babylon, city of power! (mighty city of Babylon)! In one hour, your doom has come!'" —Revelation 18:10 (NIV)

This gives us an incredible amount of specific information. Look at it closely, "will stand far off" and destroyed in "one hour", there is no doubt what this is. Three times we will hear the same term, "stand far off." There is only one thing this could be. If there is any doubt about what this is telling us, the doubt will be removed by the fact it will be repeated three times.

"The merchants who sold these things and gained their wealth from her will stand far off . . ." — Revelation 18:15 (NIV)

A second reference to "stand far off":

"In one hour such great wealth has been brought to ruin!' "Every sea captain, and all who travel by ship, the sailors, and all who earn their living from the sea, will stand far off." — Revelation 18:17 (NIV)

For the third time, "stand far off," this has to be a nuclear device which detonates over the city. The fallout from the radiation is what they will have to stand far off from. It could have no other meaning. The reference to the sea captains identifies the city as a coastal city.

"Then I heard another voice from heaven say: 'Come out of her, my people,' so that you will not share in her sins, so that you will not receive any of her plagues; 5 for her sins are piled up to heaven, and God has remembered her crimes." — Revelation 18:4 (NIV)

God's people who live in New York City have been warned to get out. Heed God's warning or you will pay the price. Meaning can be put to this prophecy. Meaning is supposed to be put to it. Those who will listen will listen. Those who won't will be destroyed with the city.

"Therefore in one day her plagues will overtake her: death, mourning and famine. She will be consumed by fire, for mighty is the Lord God who judges her." 9 "When the kings of the earth who committed adultery with her and shared her luxury see the smoke of her burning, they will weep and mourn over her." — Revelation 18:8 (NIV)

Read these words carefully: "in one day . . . consumed by fire"

Repeatedly and with great description, the books of Jeremiah and Revelation are giving us information about what will happen to New York City. Over and over. Because of endless amounts of false narratives from our institutional churches, these passages have been hidden. "Consumed by fire"

Only one thing can consume an entire city by fire in one day!

Meaning has been put to this prophecy. Heed the warning.

"While you were watching, a rock was cut out, but not by human hands. It struck the statue on its feet of iron and clay and smashed them." — Daniel 2:34 (NIV)

The "iron and clay" is a reference to the fourth beast of Daniel. It has been identified. It is the United States. We have already described what happens to New York City. It will be destroyed by a nuclear device. Meaning can now be put to this verse in Daniel. It is yet again more evidence God has given us.

The "rock not made by human hands" indeed was not made by human hands. The rock is uranium. The material which will be used to destroy New York City.

The Bible actually gives us information on the delivery method of the weapon and the geographic location of the location.

"Then a mighty angel picked up a boulder the size of a large mill-stone and threw it into the sea, and said: "With such violence the great city of Babylon will be thrown down, never to be found again." — Revelation 18:21 (NIV)

This is the delivery method. "Threw it into the sea" means the weapon won't be smuggled into the city or be a "suitcase bomb" or a dirty bomb. This will be a nuclear weapon delivered by a ballistic missile. It could have no other meaning. Notice the similarity between this verse and the verse in Daniel. Boulder size of a large millstone and "rock was cut out, but not by human hands."

"The second angel sounded his trumpet, and something like a huge mountain, all ablaze, was thrown into the sea. A third of the sea turned into blood, 9 a third of the living creatures in the sea died, and a third of the ships were destroyed." — Revelation 8:8 (NIV)

This is a tremendous passage. This passage is directly tied to all these other verses describing the fate of New York City. The mountain of fire thrown into the sea (sea of people) is the detonation of the nuclear device. The third of the ships will give us information of ground zero of the detonation. The ships are in New York Harbor. The bomb will detonate over the southwestern section of the city.

"When they see the smoke of her burning, they will exclaim, 'Was there ever a city like this great city?'" — Revelation 18:18 (NIV)

It was.

CHAPTER 19

Satan is Chained Up

Satan or the "spirit of Satan" is far more complex than we have been taught. In the simplistic view of Satan, we will miss why we are here and our rebellion. The concept itself of the devil has been taught drastically different over the generations. Not only just over time but between religions. The Jewish faith teaches Satan not strictly as a singular entity but as "the spirit of Satan." Yes, Satan the entity does exist. He and his angels get thrown out of Heaven in the end days. The Bible told us this. There is no interpretation needed for this. We are told that. Our institutional church needs to spin those verses to fit Satan into a false narrative. The "spirit of Satan" has been on this planet since Genesis. It is us. We are the serpent; we are the spirit of Satan the Bible speaks about. In the incorrect overly simplistic view about Satan, we will never see what this book in Revelation is telling us. Never.

We have seen how the institutional church has spun the hell out of Ezekiel chapter 28 and Revelation chapter 12 to fit Satan into the false narrative. By teaching Satan in the way the institutional church does, it removes our guilt and our rebellion and makes us innocent victims. We are born innocent and will have to find God through no fault of our own. This cannot be true. It describes an uncaring, unloving and cruel God and not to mention unfair.

I cannot deny the entity of Satan. That entity is the Archaios serpent in Revelation 12. The original serpent. Before the foundation of the planet is when this entity rebelled against our Creator. That made him the Archaios serpent. We were part of that rebellion. It's why we are here.

I have asked many church leaders over the years where this conflicts with any scripture. Or anything else in my first book, this book or any other statement made along these premises. The answer I have received is absolutely astounding. While they admit they don't conflict with scripture, they say it conflicts with "established doctrine." This statement alone is very telling. Today's institutional doctrine cannot be supported. Not without denigrating our Creator. This denigration is what Apostle John spoke of in his letters. It is the spirit of antichrist. Today's established doctrine teaches us of a mythical man, the antichrist, who will influence the entire planet and make people worship him. He will make people take a mark in order to buy and sell. This is completely false. There is no such man. It is such a travesty what our institutional church has done to God's Word.

"And I saw an angel coming down out of heaven, having the key to the Abyss and holding in his hand a great chain. 2 He seized the dragon, that ancient serpent, who is the devil, or Satan, and bound him for a thousand years. 3 He threw him into the Abyss, and locked and sealed it over him, to keep him from deceiving the nations anymore until the thousand years were ended. After that, he must be set free for a short time." — Revelation 20:1 (NIV)

When did Satan, the Archaios serpent, arrive on the planet? According to the institutional church "established doctrine," Satan the entity was here since Genesis; he, the serpent, tempted Eve and then had his legs removed by God. Now snakes crawl on the ground. Every time we see a snake this is supposed to remind us of God? Satan then was booted out of the Garden. They tell us this comes from Ezekiel chapter 28. This is all false. The serpent in the Garden was us, and King Tyrus was not Satan; he was a man, just a man like us. This throws off the entire Christian established doctrine. We are saved by faith not knowledge. Otherwise, no one would be saved.

Satan does not arrive on this planet until Revelation 12:7.

7 "Then war broke out in heaven. Michael and his angels fought against the dragon, and the dragon and his angels fought back. 8 But he was not strong enough, and they lost their place in heaven. 9 The great dragon was hurled down—that ancient serpent called the devil, or Satan, who leads the whole world astray. He was hurled to the earth, and his angels with him." (NIV)

From Revelation chapter 12, we know who the woman was, the one in the pain of child birth. The institutional church doctrine says it is Israel, and the child is Christ. How could that be? How would that support Satan being cast out of the Garden if that child is Christ? In that false interpretation, Satan would have arrived on the scene thousands of years ago. After all, according to Revelation chapter 12, the serpent does not get cast down until the woman goes into the pain of childbirth. If the child is Christ, it will throw off the timing by thousands of years. Under the established doctrine, the timing is thrown off by thousands of years. It's an inconvenient question which will go unanswered by the institutional church leaders. As in many other questions, it is not even allowed to be asked. Satan did not get thrown out of Heaven in the time of Christ, nor did he get thrown out of Heaven in the book of Genesis. When Satan spoke to God in the book of Job and again to Jesus in the gospel, he had not yet been thrown out of Heaven. He was in the spirit and thus very limited to what he could do here on this Earth. Limited by God as we saw in the book of Job. Satan has no authority. Satan arrives here in the last days, which means there are two different serpents. The spirit of Satan (us), and Satan the entity. Satan has never been linked with us as God has not, for the same reason. We have to live on this Earth of our own accord. Unbiased by God and unbiased by Satan. If this were not the case God would show himself to us directly. Ever wonder why He hasn't? He is the Creator of the universe. If He wanted to prove His existence to us, it would not be beyond His capabilities. He has not because we have to live in the rebellion we asked for. Satan as well cannot directly influence us outside of our own natures. That would throw off the rational for why we are here as well. Christ died because of us not just for us. He died because we rebelled against God before the foundation of the planet. It's why we are here. The only unjust influence on us is us and not Satan. In this "experiment," God has allowed us to live without Him. We have no one to blame for it, not Adam and Eve, not Satan, not a false church or false prophets, just us. Our nature is our nature. Satan does not arrive here until Revelation chapter 12.

Yes, Satan came with the angels in the book of Job. Not in the flesh but in the same spirit of the angels. God asked him where he came from; Satan's reply was a direct blasphemy to God. "I go to and fro on the Earth and walk up and down on the face of it." That reference is about us; we are the ones walking to and fro on the Earth not Satan himself. In the exchange between God and Satan, immediately after, Satan says he goes to and fro on the planet. God asks Satan about Job. In this passage in Job, chapter 1 and verses 7 and 8 are directly tied to each other. Satan told God the spirit of the rebellion, us humans, roamed the Earth. Gods question to Satan about Job was in response to Satan's statement. Satan was not on the planet in the physical realm.

When Satan spoke to Jesus and tempted him, he was asking him to join him and to join us in the rebellion. Satan was not here in the flesh, not yet. God has not allowed Satan to directly intervene in our lives. But something else does, the serpent in our natures, the rebellious nature which made us fall. When Jesus told Peter, "get behind me Satan," he was talking to Peter. That "Satan" was the serpent in Peter's nature. That rebellious nature.

In Corinthians, Paul told husbands and wives to submit to each other so that "Satan" doesn't tempt them. That Satan is not the Archaios Serpent, Lucifer or the devil. That "Satan" is the serpent in our nature; it's us. If wives don't submit to their husbands the temptation does not come from Satan, it comes from lust and desire in our own nature. The entity of Satan, the devil does not have that ability, God could not allow it. If that were the case, we would have no purpose here on this Earth. Satan does not have that link to us, yet, but he will here in this verse. Satan will be cast out of Heaven; when that happens, it will be quite literally Hell here on Earth.

In the gospel of John, Jesus said:

8:44 "You belong to your father, the devil, and you want to carry out your father's desires. He was a murderer from the beginning, not holding to the truth, for there is no truth in him. When he lies, he speaks his native language, for he is a liar and the father of lies." (NIV)

Who was this man's father? What was Jesus saying? Who did Satan murder? Was Cain Satan? This is a reference to the spirit of Satan, our fallen nature. Cain killed Abel not the devil. This man

Jesus spoke to was not reconciled with God. That was the reference Jesus was making. This man was not reconciled and therefore his "father"; his affiliation was to the nature of the rebellion. This man was living in his rebellion. That is what Jesus was saying. In the simplistic false narrative of Satan from the institutional church, this verse has no meaning.

"I saw thrones on which were seated those who had been given authority to judge. And I saw the souls of those who had been beheaded because of their testimony about Jesus and because of the word of God. They had not worshiped the beast or its image and had not received its mark on their foreheads or their hands. They came to life and reigned with Christ a thousand years." — Revelation 20:4 (NIV)

These men did not worship the beast or take the number of his name. That's true they didn't, they couldn't; they were already dead. From earlier in Revelation we were told the 144,000 were "redeemed from the Earth." They had lived and died and were brought back to life. Those in verse four "came to life"; they as well had lived, died and came back to life. They did not take the mark of the beast because they did not come from our time. This verse does not tell us they refused the mark; it is telling us they came from our past. They could not have taken the mark. They died a long time ago. These men are not us. If you are alive today as part of the rebellion, you will not reign with Christ during the thousand-year reign. The next verse tells us this.

"(The rest of the dead did not come to life until the thousand years were ended.) This is the first resurrection. 6 Blessed and holy are those who share in the first resurrection. The second death has no power over them, but they will be priests of God and of Christ and will reign with him for a thousand years." — Revelation 20:5 (NIV)

The rest of the dead is the rest of us. We will not reign with Christ in this thousand year. The spirit of Satan nor will the entity Satan have a presence on this planet.

CHAPTER 20:

The Myth of
Established Doctrine

Some time ago, a vocal critic of *Cursed Above All Cattle* said to me that the facts in the book were false. She is an adamant member of the institutional church. Her premise was that there is this thing called "commonality of the spirit." My apparent violation was that I went against established doctrine. According to her, since we have one Bible and one God, we have a "commonality of the spirit" which means established doctrine is correct doctrine. This leads me to many questions she would not answer; after all, she refused to read the book and would not support her doctrine, nor would she let me explain the doctrine in the book.

History of man on this planet will prove commonality of the spirit, of man's spirit has been wrong from the beginning. Where was the "commonality of the spirit" when all but eight people were killed in the flood? Certainly, the 99% could not have been wrong according to the premise that the majority is always right. The majority has to have the preponderance of the truth because it is what the tribal rules dictate. That seems to never be the case. Man has been wrong from the beginning. Isaiah gave us an indication of this in Isaiah 29:13, God said, "You worship me with your mouth . . . your hearts are far from me . . . you worship me in man's truth." Where was this "commonality of the spirit" then? When Christ gave His testimony, He was thoroughly rejected by the institutional leadership. Again, where was that commonality then? Was their established doctrine correct because it was common? Jesus corrected them on false doctrine. I put this question to an IC leader. He told me Christ changed all this. Many believe this today. If this is the case, then how is it the disciples and apostles were imprisoned, tortured and killed? So, when did Jesus "change" all this? The largest IC on the planet believed the Earth was flat and the center of the universe four hundred years ago. That certainly was after the death of Christ. Was it changed then? If not, how could established doctrine been so far of? The Catholic Church would imprison people if not kill them for heresy if they dissented with this false doctrine. This "commonality of the spirit" is what men of the IC say to defend the established doctrine as true. It is not. Man is wrong. This is the discontinuity of man.

"Man" has had it wrong from the beginning. Today's institutional churches are teaching man's truth, not God's truth. What they say with their mouths are not what they describe with their actions. They say God is a God of love with their mouth but then describe God as an evil heartless Creator who would create a planet in which He would condemn the majority to Hell. Billions and billions of people.

God told us this would happen.

"For the time will come when people will not put up with sound doctrine. Instead, to suit their own desires, they will gather around

them a great number of teachers to say what their itching ears want to hear. 4They will turn their ears away from the truth and turn aside to myths." — 2nd Timothy 4:3 (NIV)

"They exchanged the truth about God for a lie, and worshiped and served created things rather than the Creator — who is forever praised. Amen." — Romans 1:25(NIV)

This is where our IC lives today. They have exchanged the truth about God with a lie. They are tickling ears and teaching myths. We will take a close look at the established doctrines.

Myth #1: Satan took the form of an animal in the Garden of Eden.

The story from the IC: Satan took the form of a beautiful animal in the Garden and tempted Eve to disobey God. God got mad at this animal and ripped its legs off and turned it into a snake. When we see snakes today slivering on the ground it is a reminder to us of the rebellion of Adam and Eve. They get this from Genesis 3:14.

"Cursed are you above all livestock and all wild animals! You will crawl on your belly and you will eat dust all the days of your life." (NIV)

They also use Ezekiel 28. Even though God told us three times King Tyre was a mortal man, the IC twists King Tyre into Satan.

Let's poke holes in this myth being taught as a staple of today's established truth.

Why would God get angry with an animal being used by Satan? Punish the animal but not punish Satan? This animal now, without legs, was somehow able to procreate with a like species of which their offspring no longer had legs? So, in addition to God ripping its legs off, He had also changed this animal's DNA. He would have had to; after all, lots of our veterans come back from war with missing body parts; they procreate and have children with all of their limbs. So why would God do this?

I had often wondered why IC members today cannot make the shift to an old Earth and defer to science on the age of the Earth as we did with its shape. They cannot without creating a big problem. If they were to change their thinking, in addition to admitting to teaching false doctrine, it would also necessitate a shift to the myth of this animal. You see, the same science telling us the planet is 4.5 billion years old is also telling us snakes have been crawling on their bellies for millions of years. From the genealogy in the Bible we can determine Adam and Eve were created about six thousand years ago. We have a conflict. It's a paradox. One of the many which cannot be answered without lying about God.

Let's look at what really happened. God did not rip off an animal's legs or change any DNA. The serpent God was talking to was us. We are the serpent God was speaking to. Now Ezekiel 28 will now make sense and not conflict with the rest of the scripture. The curse is our nature, our rebellious nature against Him. Why would He say "you are cursed above all cattle?" Snakes are not mammals; we are. That curse was aimed at us. "You will crawl on your bellies" is a derogatory reference to our sexual nature. Now there is no paradox; now there is no conflict with the physical properties of our universe, and now this verse fits. We are not innocent.

Myth #2: Our spiritual creation happened at our physical birth.

The story from the IC:

Our souls (spirits) are created at our physical birth. We are born innocent and will spend eternity with God if we die before we reach the age of accountability or if we reconcile with God before we die. As we spelled out earlier in the book, this would make God either incompetent or heartless. Regardless of what the IC says with their mouths, they are describing a God who is cruel and heartless. Another paradox.

This myth conflicts with Ephesians 1:4, which is a verse they need to spin and change to a meaningless verse.

"For he chose us in Him before the creation of the world to be holy and blameless in His sight. In love." (NIV)

What really happened?

We were with God before the foundation of the Earth and we rebelled against Him which is why we are here. We need to reconcile to God because of this rebellion and no other. There is no paradox as to the nature of God. We are not innocent. God loves us and always has even after we rebelled against Him.

No paradox. This may conflict with established doctrine, but it will not conflict with scripture. Not one word in scripture supports the established doctrine, not one word. It is also why God does not show His presence to us directly.

Myth #3: We pay for the Sin of Adam and Eve.

The story from the IC:

Eve was tempted by Satan and caused Adam to disobey God with her. After which mankind lived separated from God and all mankind needed to reconcile with God because of their disobedience. This is a paradox. God created us but does not directly communicate with us or show Himself directly to us but expects us to see His created works and make our way back to Him because of it. Most will not. That is a paradox. If God put us here to reconcile with Him, one might think God would be more proactive in His proof to us of His existence. If the IC premise was correct, God would bring down angels in our presence so they could speak to us. So, we could see them and have proof. Has anyone in the IC answered this paradox? Instead, our leaders claim a direct communication with God. They say "God whispered in my ear" or God spoke to my heart." The parishioners may not feel this or hear this voice so they will defer to the men that make such a claim. Or in many cases they will parrot the claims of the others saying such things. Job's friends did this. When Job was being tested by God, Job's friends claimed a moral superiority and even made claim that God spoke to them directly. They were lying as are our IC leaders, many of them. At no point in the Bible is there proof that God spoke to man in the plurality being claimed today. God did speak to men in the Bible. Never for their own glory but for the will and glory of God. Look at the apostles and the disciples of Jesus. Then think of today's well-known church leaders. They live in mansions and fly private jets. How does that compare to those men of old? Nothing has changed. Matthew 23 still applies. We are being lied to. God is not speaking to their hearts. If so, they would not spew obscuration and put themselves above one another. They also would not be quenching the spirit because it opposes their false doctrine.

The truth:

Adam and Eve did sin against God, as was preplanned before the foundation of the planet. Adam and Eve did bring sin (the rebellion against God) into the world. They did not bring our sin. We do not pay for the sin of Adam and Eve; we pay for our own sin, our own rebellion against God which happened long before our physical birth. It happened before the foundation of the planet. If this were not the case, then we would have the same direct knowledge of God Adam and Eve had. Their direct descendants also had this knowledge, assuming Adam and Eve spoke to their kids. God spoke directly to Cain. If our eternity hinges on our belief in God and our belief in Jesus, you would think we would be afforded the same opportunity. This can be answered under the correct premise. No paradox.

Myth #4: The enmity of Genesis is between Satan and Christ.

The story from the IC:

God put enmity between Satan and Christ.

"And I will put enmity between you and the woman, and between your offspring and hers; he will crush your head, and you will strike his heel." — Genesis 3:15 (NIV)

This enmity is between Christ and Satan; his "offspring" are the spiritual offspring of Satan as referenced in John 8:44, "your father the serpent." The woman is Israel and her offspring are Christ. Jesus will crush the head of the serpent.

There are holes in this belief aside from there is no scriptural support for it. The spiritual opposition between God and Satan started before the foundation of the planet; remember, salvation through Christ was planned before the Earth was formed. So why would God "put" enmity between two opposing spiritual forces at this point in time? Why would offspring mean two different things in the same verse? One is a spiritual offspring, and the other is a physical one. Is the IC really going to tell us we are the physical descendants of Satan? Will they tell us Satan procreated? It's a paradox.

The truth:

The enmity is between male and female. God put this in as a protection. The difference lies in the different natures. Females, by nature, will categorize men into procreation and resource men. Often it will not be the same man. This is not taught in church or in Bible study. Christians will never mention it because it seems to be a very derogatory part of the female nature. They will assign character issues to a female who cheats on her husband but not an issue with her nature. This thing in the female nature is why men are surprised when they find their wife, who may be completely sexually inhibited around them, are not in the least sexually inhibited around other men. Females by nature are not monogamous. It's in their nature to categorize men in these different ways. The stronger male or the man in which she may identify an attribute she does not find in her husband, she will not be sexually inhibited with that man. That trait is in the female nature whether we agree with it or not. Politically correct or not. None the less, it is there. Men do not have that trait. Men are also non-monogamous by nature but in an entirely different way. The thing in the female nature which categorizes men into procreation and resource men do not have. Men do not categorize females in this way. The sexual motivation in the male nature is completely different than in the female's nature. Apostle Paul knew this.

"Now for the matters you wrote about: "It is good for a man not to have sexual relations with a woman." 2 But since sexual immorality is occurring, each man should have sexual relations with his own wife, and each woman with her own husband." —1st Corinthians 7:1 (NIV)

Paul knew about our nature and he knew about the enmity. These verses in Corinthians are a mitigation strategy against this nature. First, he says not to have a sexual relationship and presumably remain single which would be the ultimate enmity mitigation strategy of all. It takes the enmity completely out of the picture. The second one is to marry and sexually submit to each other.

The enmity does protect us from something. It prevents us from replacing God with the connection we could have with our wives if not for the enmity and the constant force in our different natures to struggle for the control in our relationships. It's why after the initial stage of our marriages, we struggle with all those things married people constantly struggle with. The enmity is what prevents us from replacing God.

The enmity is between male and female. Existing due to our different natures. Our marriages are not what the institutional church has taught us.

Myth #5: The age of the planet is six thousand years old.

The story from the IC:

God made the Earth in six calendar days and rested on the seventh. The planet and all that is on it has only been around for six thousand years. The genealogy in the Old Testament pinpoints the creation of Adam and Eve to be six thousand years ago. Since the Earth was created in six calendar days, the Earth itself would have to be six thousand years old.

"In the beginning God created the heavens and the earth. 2 Now the earth was formless and empty, darkness was over the surface of the deep, and the Spirit of God was hovering over the waters." – Genesis 1:1–2 (NIV)

Even though God made the Earth, and His Spirit moved over the face of the deep, there was no time lapse between verse 1 and 3. God only moved over the Earth for one day. The Earth wasn't formless and empty very long, just a day before everything started. We won't dwell on the fact the vegetation was made on day three and the sun was made on day 4; it produced after its own kind without the sun.

All the ancient dinosaurs lived within this last six-thousand-year period. Even the Tyrannosaurus. The fact that fossils were uncovered below millions of years of sediment and that scientists can track the lineage of these species; they are only six thousand years old. The flood in the time of Noah wiped them out. Carbon dating and radiometric dating are unproven sciences which are flawed; it has to be, or our interpretation of Genesis 1 would have to be incorrect. We know our interpretations of the Bible are never incorrect because we are man; we are never wrong. Yes, the Scribes and Pharisees were wrong about some of the commandments, and the church in the time of Isaiah 29:13 was wrong, but that was them not us. Yes, the church four hundred years ago misinterpreted Genesis 1:14–16 and thought the Earth was flat and the center of the universe, but they were wrong, and we are correct in our interpretation of Genesis 1. Please discard all the science they teach you in school. All of it has to be wrong because it disagrees with our interpretation. We are the institutional church leader; we have the preponderance of the truth.

The truth:

For many generations entire religious organizations have been formed to dispute the science from the secular world. As science has advanced and been refined, so have these religious organizations. These organizations have never been seeking the truth, and their goal is to dispute the truth. Because of the arrogance and self-righteousness of man, they believe they already have the truth and therefore will not listen or do they have the ability to change. Very similar to the church four hundred years ago holding on to false interpretation, today's institutional church is doing the same. They will twist the very physical characteristics of the universe in order to not accept the fact Genesis was misinterpreted.

Debating science with church members is futile. We know how the debate goes. We know the talking points which will be thrown out. I will not enter into a debate with the spiritually blind. They will either see, or they will not. They will see what the prophecies are, or they will not.

The Earth is 4.5 billion years old. The seven days in Genesis was not seven calendar days. Science is not wrong or off 99%. The reassembled tyrannosaurus displayed in the American Museum of Natural History in New York City is not six thousand years old. Not even close. It's estimated at sixty-five million years old. That's a big difference. The conflict isn't between God and science. It's between science and false doctrine. Yet again.

Myth #6: The antichrist is a man.

The story from the IC:

In the end days, this man will come along and rule the planet. He will be a man possessed by Satan. People will worship him. He will be very powerful and make people worship the beast, and he will make people take a mark on their right hand or on their forehead. You must take the mark of the beast in order to buy and sell. If you take this mark, you fail God's litmus test and will be doomed to Hell.

The truth:

This is a complete lie. All the verses the IC uses to support this nonsense are not valid. Apostle John tells us the "spirit" of antichrist will come along in the end days. It is here. It was then, and it is now. The institutional church speaks of a loving God but describes to us a cruel hateful God when it tells us God created billions of people He would condemn to Hell. This is not the case. Their doctrine cannot be supported. Today's institutional church is the" antichrist spirit" John warned us about. They are telling us lies and myths about God, as we were told they would. The narrative of the antichrist is a complete lie. The IC is indeed leading many astray.

Myth #7: In the end days, you must refuse the mark of the beast.

The story from the IC:

In the end days, a beast will come along and make the inhabitants of the Earth to take this mark. You must take it in order to buy and sell. If you take it, you will be lost to God. It is a litmus test for the end day believers. The beast will use this to cause people on this planet to "worship him" or die.

The truth:

This is completely false. We are the ones who did not have our names written in the book of life before the foundation of the planet. We will all take the mark of the beast. The beast is not the antichrist. Not even close. The beast in Revelation is the United States. The "image" of the beast will be our new currency. It will change when the United States "sets up an image of the beast," which means, it will switch our currency from the current fiat-based money to an electronic currency. This will be necessary due to the reckless economic policies which have put our economy in ruin. The image of the beast being able to speak means the currency will be driven by current technology. Not black magic.

These myths are endless. The "commonality of the spirit" which supports the "established doctrine" in itself is false doctrine. The entire institutional church has led the entire planet astray by telling lies and myths about God.

"Many will come in my name, claiming to be messiah, and lead many astray." Jesus told us this would happen. It has.

CHAPTER 21

The Lie of Eliphaz

12 "A word was secretly brought to me, my ears caught a whisper of it. 13 Amid disquieting dreams in the night, when deep sleep falls on people, 14 fear and trembling seized me and made all my bones shake. 15 A spirit glided past my face, and the hair on my body stood on end. 16 It stopped, but I could not tell what it was. A form stood before my eyes, and I heard a hushed voice: 17 'Can a mortal be more righteous than God? Can even a strong man be more pure than his Maker?'" (NIV)

What communication do we have with God? Seems like a very simple question. What relationship do we actually have with God?

The above verse is from the book of Job. God allowed Satan to test Job's faith. While Job was going through the pain and the suffering of the trial, the book of Job recounts the words of three of Jobs friends: Eliphaz, Bildad and Zophar.

These three friends had no idea that God was allowing Satan to test Job. So, each took turns giving Job council. Essentially their council to Job is that he must have done something to God to invoke God's anger. Eliphaz in his arrogance and self-righteousness told Job that his affliction was caused or made worse due to Job complaining about his suffering. Eliphaz, Bildad and Zophar had no idea what they were talking about, but they spoke with definiteness. They spoke with absolute assuredness when they spoke for God. They looked down on Job and scolded and scorned him.

There are very remarkable points on this. It's extremely important to understand something. The understanding of this passage in Job will lead to the understanding of how today's church has gone astray. We have a world full of Eliphaz's and Diotrephes's who are claiming a communication with God which does not exist. Claiming a relationship with God which does not exist. They do this for their glory not God's. They do this for commercial gain and to increase their status, all the while destroying God's Word.

In order to make his case against Job, Eliphaz made the above statement in Job 4. He made a statement that God spoke to him directly through the Spirit. Eliphaz did this to prove his case. His case was false against Job; therefore, the statement he made about the communication from the Spirit was also false. It is not to say the Spirit does not speak to us, and yes usually in the early morning hours (the cool of the day), but when it does, it's for God's glory and not ours. It is certainly not for use in an argument to prove yourself correct as Eliphaz did.

It is extremely important to understand something. If we look in the popular modern-day Bible commentaries, none of them will say Eliphaz was lying or making something up to improve his status or to solidify his case. The commentaries written by man will only go so far as to say that Eliphaz was mistaken. He didn't clearly understand his vision or had misapplied his vision to Job's circumstance. Think about this. If this were true, why would this passage be written in the Bible? What statement would God be making? That a true man of God, Eliphaz, just made a mistake? Misapplied a vision? That is nonsensical. Why would God do that? He didn't. The statement God made to us was far deeper. Today's institutional church will stay far, far away from this passage.

Eliphaz was lying. He relayed this story for his own glory. By spewing this lie, who would contest him? As the Bible commentaries mentioned, Eliphaz did not say anything contrary about God or anything that would conflict with the scripture, so the institutional church will excuse Eliphaz and say he was just mistaken. We have to go back to what was just said. Why would this passage be in God's Word if this were the case? Why did the Bible not mention this? It didn't tell us Eliphaz made a mistake or misunderstood the vision. It is not what happened, and today's institutional church and all the biblical commentaries are hiding this from us. Eliphaz lied. He did it to increase his own standing, credibility and status.

Today's IC covers for the lie because they are all doing the same thing. They claim these direct communications with God as Eliphaz did, for the same reasons. It's great for their own glory, status, commercial success and standing. They do not say things against established doctrine, or their lie would not work, and they would be exposed for who they are. God is not talking with today's Laodicean church leaders. God told us He would spew them out of His mouth. And yet they stand up in front of their parishioners and proclaim, "God spoke to my heart."

We have a massive problem today with something. If a church leader does not lie, they will not have a very big business. If they are honest, they will not generate interest among those looking to have their ears tickled. So, they are forced to lie. The other part of this huge problem is that the concept of this direct communication has worked its way into today's tribalism. People believe something which is not true.

God never speaks to us for our glory. Never. God speaks to us for His glory. Which is why we don't say "God spoke to us."

Because of this false tribalistic belief, much false doctrine is being spread. It's why no one is reading *Cursed Above All Cattle* and possibly won't read this book either. These two books completely unlock the prophecies, but as of now, have generated little interest. That is how strong tribalism is. It has a grip on this planet.

If we remove ourselves from tribalism and really look at our communication with God and with Satan, then we will really see ourselves.

God's intervention in our lives is for His glory or for our mercy. We live in our rebellion, so we cannot claim anything other.

There is a misconception about our communication with God. There is also a misconception about the influence Satan has over our lives.

If you believe today's leaders, it seems that they have this direct two-way communication with God. We know what they say and the euphemisms they use. We have all heard it a million times. They are lying as Eliphaz was. I heard one of these leaders once say, "God spoke to me and told me to show authority," and he actually said that to his congregation. God spoke to him and gave him a specific word "authority." Think about that statement. God told a man to show authority. Whose glory was that for? People follow this man. By lying about this communication with God, this man has greatly damaged the Word for his own personal gain.

God does not intervene in our lives as these men claim. God allows us to live in our rebellion. It's why we are here. If God did intervene as they claim, why would a tornado strike a church and kill church members or how could a van full of kids going to Bible camp crash and kill all on board? God answers prayers which He told us He would. Prayers do get answered. God does not otherwise directly intervene in our rebellion for the same reason He does not directly show Himself or His angels to us. God will communicate with us for His purpose not ours.

"or because of these surpassingly great revelations. Therefore, in order to keep me from becoming conceited, I was given a thorn in my flesh, a messenger of Satan, to torment me. 8 Three times I pleaded with the Lord to take it away from me. 9 But he said to me, "My grace is sufficient for you, for my power is made perfect in weakness." Therefore I will boast all the more gladly about my weaknesses, so that Christ's power may rest on me."—2nd Corinthians 12:7 (NIV)

Three times Paul asked God to remove the thorn from His side. God said no. Has anyone ever asked why? If God intervenes in our lives, and we all have this two-way direct communication with God, why are we all so far apart on doctrine and why did God say no to Paul?

In this realm, God would not intervene in Paul's life for the same reason He does not intervene in our lives. The thorn in Paul's side was put there by Paul. It was in his nature. The "Satan" in this verse was not Satan the entity. It was Paul's nature. It was Paul's motivation for his fall. That is why God would not remove it. All of us on this planet have our own motivations for our fall. God does not intervene or live our life for us. He is allowing us to live apart from Himself because we asked for it. If He intervened or communicated with us constantly it would throw His plan for us off. There is no doubt that God has the right to speak to us in any manner

He pleases and has no restrictions in that regard. We don't choose that, nor should we claim we attain it as Eliphaz did. By doing so, it causes a massive disruption within the body of Christ. It drives our current tribalism.

Today it is acceptable and even required to claim that direct communication with God. God does work in our lives but not in the way it is advertised.

Satan has little to no influence over us. Satan and his angels have been on the sidelines since the beginning. He does not get thrown out of Heaven until the end. All this time he has been accusing us before God, day and night. The only Satan driving this planet is our own nature. The "spirit of Satan" we were born into.

When the COVID-19 virus was released on the planet, a church leader came on television and spoke to it. He said in an impassioned voice with great emotion, "God is with us; He will fight this virus with us." That man was lying. God could, in a single second, wipe this virus out with a single command. He has not. He does not intervene unless it's for His will. God is not our "ally." He does not intervene in the rebellion we asked for. That man did what all of our institutional church leaders do. He spoke for God with no wisdom of who we are and why we are here.

Yet another one of these leaders declared on his blog: "God will crush the evil head of racism," that man is lying. At any second God could end this planet and end all the pain and suffering but He has not. He is not our ally. He answers prayers. He is not our ally, nor does He intervene in our lives outside of His prerogative.

This statement of truth violates the rules of today's institutional church tribalism. This tribalism is where our church lives today.

It is where the Scribes and Pharisees lived. It is where man has always lived.

CHAPTER 22

What Church?

14 *"They raise their voices, they shout for joy; from the west they acclaim the LORD's majesty. 15 Therefore in the east give glory to the LORD; exalt the name of the LORD, the God of Israel, in the islands of the sea."*

16 *"From the ends of the earth we hear singing: 'Glory to the Righteous One.' But I said, 'I waste away, I waste away! Woe to me! The treacherous betray! With treachery the treacherous betray!'"*

These are two very different places. Verse 14 and 15 are the "islands in the sea." They are the invisible church, the remnant and the body of Christ. They exalt God. They belong to God.

Verse 16 is not the body of Christ. They talk like they are, they appear to exalt God; they do not. They exalt man. This is the Laodicean church. The lukewarm church. This is today's Christian organizational churches. All denominations. In this place, men exalt themselves. Men claim to speak for God; they write books and run their carnival shows in which they charge a fee for the attendees. They say "God spoke to me" or "God spoke to my heart" and then spew out obscuration. They are religious men of wealth and status. The world loves them. In this place, they "sell" the salvation prayer which removes the fear of eternity without God. It removes the guilt. They cite the thief on the cross. Be like him and you will receive eternal life. They meet once a week and sing. They say, "Glory to the Righteous one."

But how do they live? Do they go back to their high mortgage homes, expensive cars and the college debt for their children? Do the live-in pursuit of the worldly status? Is God in the forefront of their lives? Or is that just on Sunday?

Matthew 24

23 "At that time if anyone says to you, 'Look, here is the Messiah!' or, 'There he is!' do not believe it."

24 "For false messiahs and false prophets will appear and perform great signs and wonders to deceive, if possible, even the elect."

25 "See, I have told you ahead of time."

26 "So if anyone tells you, 'There he is, out in the wilderness,' do not go out; or, 'Here he is, in the inner rooms,' do not believe it."

28 "Wherever there is a carcass, there the vultures will gather."

Today, this passage in Matthew is very important and relevant. This prophecy is currently underway; believers need to beware.

On the surface, it might seem I am judging or criticizing our leaders. I have been accused of that behavior a lot from my writings. It is not a judgment. It is identifying what Jesus told us to what is actually happening today.

Jesus gave us the above passage. We are not being judgmental or critical by marrying up the prophecy he gave us to current day events. Not at all. We are just putting meaning to this prophecy. Our leaders today fulfil this prophecy. They are is claiming to be speaking for God, even though they are not. Many are doing this. Today's leaders, well known and respected, are doing the same thing. Some may be more refined than others, but are still fulfilling this prophecy. When they preach the false narratives of the established Christian doctrines, like the enmity is between Satan and Christ or that a man, the antichrist, will come along in the end days, they are lying. Their doctrine is a lie against God; they are leading the planet astray in order for the world to love them enough to sell many books and other profit generations. They are the ones in this passage in Matthew. The entire Christian organization of today is the Laodicean church. Little of what you hear on Sunday is useful information about God, about us, about how we are really told to live and about what it truly means to reconcile with God. The planet is being led astray.

Over 2.5 billion men are about to die on this planet. They will be killed by the COVID-19 vaccine. It was caused by man. It is a judgment from God but made by the evil of man. Nothing could have stopped this because it was prophesied. It was not a matter of awareness; God could have done that. Our Christian leaders have lied to us. They claim a connection to God they do not have; none of us have that connection for our own glory. When God speaks to us, it is for His glory.

Our leaders have profited by their claim. They tell people to recite the "salvation" prayer and join their church. They take away your fear but teach things that are in man's truth. They tell you: you can be blessed and prosperous. Because that's what God does, gives us idols we can worship if we pay lip service to Him.

The deaths of all these men will be due to the fact this planet is living in rebellion to God. They will die because they did not listen.

The antichrist has been revealed in this book. They did not listen.

The 4th beast of Daniel was revealed in *Cursed Above All Cattle*. They did not listen.

The enmity in Genesis was revealed as was the serpent. They did not listen.

The end day prophecies were unsealed. They did not listen.

Look at these Bible verses;

"Surely you know, for you were already born! You have lived so many years!" — Job 38:21 (NIV)

"But women will be saved through childbearing — if they continue in faith, love and holiness with propriety." — 1st Timothy 2:15 (NIV)

"Or because of these surpassingly great revelations. Therefore, in order to keep me from becoming conceited, I was given a thorn in my flesh, a messenger of Satan, to torment me." — 2nd Corinthians 12:7 (NIV)

No man has put meaning to these verses.

These verses can easily be understood. They do have profound meaning. Once we leave our idols and reconcile with our Creator, we will see them. Once people leave the Laodicean doctrine, they will understand these verses. The many will not.